WRITING WITH STYLE

WRITING WITH STYLE

The Economist Guide

LANE GREENE

WRITING WITH STYLE

Published with permission from *The Economist* by Pegasus Books.

The Economist is an imprint of
Pegasus Books, Ltd.
148 West 37th Street, 13th Floor
New York, NY 10018

First Pegasus Books cloth edition July 2023

ISBN: 978-1-63936-437-4

10 9 8 7 6 5 4 3 2

Printed in the United States of America
Distributed by Simon & Schuster
www.pegasusbooks.com

PEGASUS BOOKS
NEW YORK LONDON

For Eva

ABOUT THE AUTHOR

Lane Greene is the language columnist ("Johnson") and Spain correspondent at *The Economist*. Previous assignments have included digital news, books and culture, European business, law, energy, the environment and American politics. He is based in Madrid, after being based in London, Berlin and New York. He is a recipient of the journalism award from the Linguistic Society of America and speaks nine languages.

ALSO BY THE AUTHOR

Talk on the Wild Side: Why Language Won't Do As It's Told (2018)

You Are What You Speak: Grammar Grouches, Language Laws, and the Politics of Identity (2011)

Contents

Introduction

The purpose of *The Economist* is to be clear. And clarity of writing usually follows clarity of thought. So think what you want to say, then say it as simply as you can. Keep in mind George Orwell's six rules:

1. Never use a metaphor, simile, or other figure of speech which you are used to seeing in print.
2. Never use a long word where a short one will do.
3. If it is possible to cut a word out, always cut it out.
4. Never use the passive where you can use the active.
5. Never use a foreign phrase, a scientific word, or a jargon word if you can think of an everyday English equivalent.
6. Break any of these rules sooner than say anything outright barbarous.

These rules serve different purposes:

1. Originality. *The Economist* aims to give its readers analysis they will not get elsewhere. But we also hope to compete on the quality of our writing. If readers find a familiar, overused phrase every sentence or so, their minds will wander. But if our writers arrest their attention by novelty of imagery, analogy and phrasing, reading our pages will be pleasurable, and they will read on.

2. Clarity. Articles in *The Economist* should be like essays, in that they have a beginning, a middle and an end. Each should be a coherent whole, a series of paragraphs that follow logically and, ideally, will suffer if even one sentence is cut out. If the article is a report, the facts must be selected and presented as a story. If it is a leader or more analytical article, it should also have a sense of sequence, so the reader has the feeling of being carried from a beginning to a conclusion. Either way, it is up to you to provide the ideas, analysis and argument that bind the elements of the article together. That is the hard part. Once you have them, though, you need only plain, straightforward words to express them. Short words are more than short; they are clear. The stock of short, old words in the English language has a special role in a good English sentence (about which we will hear more in Chapter 1). Use the language of everyday speech, not that of lawyers or bureaucrats. So prefer *let* to *permit*, *people* to *persons*, *buy* to *purchase*, *colleague* to *peer*, *present* to *gift*, *rich* to *wealthy*, *show* to *demonstrate*, *break* to *violate*. Pomposity and long-windedness tend to obscure meaning, or reveal the lack of it. Strip them away in favour of plain words.

3. Concision. Our readers are busy. They can be easily seduced by any other magazine or newspaper (or indeed any other app on their phones). When readers give us their time, we want to make it worthwhile, and that means making every word count.

4. Honesty. The passive has its occasional uses, but one of its chief misuses is the way in which it can conceal who did what in the sentence: remember Ronald Reagan's famous *Mistakes were made*. Active sentences can be elusive too. But if you turn as many passives into actives as you can, your writing will be more direct and more transparent.

5. Humility. Read through your writing several times. Edit it ruthlessly, whether by cutting or polishing or sharpening, on each occasion. Avoid repetition. Cut out anything superfluous. And resist the temptation to achieve a literary effect by making elliptical remarks or allusions to unexplained people or events. Rather, hold your reader's attention by keeping the story moving. If the tale begins to flag, or the arguments seem less than convincing, you can rescue it only by the sharpness of your mind.

Avoid scientific, foreign or jargon words. Jargon is often intended to show off, telling the reader that you know something special. Ideally you really do know something your reader doesn't, but putting those facts into everyday English makes your article read less like a lecture and more like an intelligent friend explaining something. It also means that you will have to be honest with yourself about what you aim to say. In plain words it is far harder to hide if you aren't sure what you mean.

Don't be hectoring or arrogant. Those who disagree with you are not necessarily *stupid* or *insane*. Nobody needs to be described as silly;

let your analysis show that instead. When you express opinions, do not simply make assertions. The aim is not just to tell readers what you think, but to persuade them. If you use arguments, reasoning and evidence, you may succeed. Go easy on *oughts* and *shoulds*.

Don't be too pleased with yourself. Don't boast of your own cleverness by telling your readers that you correctly predicted something or that you have a scoop. You are more likely to bore or irritate them than to impress them.

6. Lucidity. Simple sentences help. Keep complicated constructions and gimmicks to a minimum, if necessary by remembering the *New Yorker*'s comment: "Backward ran sentences until reeled the mind."

If your syntax is crisp, a longer sentence now and again will not over-tax the reader. Remember Mark Twain's advice on how a writer treats sentences: "At times he may indulge himself with a long one, but he will make sure there are no folds in it, no vaguenesses, no parenthetical interruptions of its view as a whole; when he has done with it, it won't be a sea-serpent with half of its arches under the water; it will be a torch-light procession." A sentence without discipline is not a torch-light procession, but a torch-bearing mob.

Twain, like Orwell, was a great stylist. Of another writer, he said that he "hadn't any more invention than a horse; and I don't mean a high-class horse, either; I mean a clothes-horse." Twain's rules for writers echo Orwell's. He said that a writer should:

- Say what he is proposing to say, not merely come near it.
- Use the right word, not its second cousin.
- Eschew surplusage.
- Not omit necessary details.
- Avoid slovenliness of form.
- Use good grammar.
- Employ a simple and straightforward style.

Easily said. But what are the right words? Good grammar? Simple style?

What follows are rules like Orwell's and Twain's, discovered by good writers again and again, with a dash of what *The Economist*'s own scribblers have discovered over 180 years and counting.

part 1

The big things

1

Old and short: words

The Economist's philosophy on vocabulary can be summed up in a quote from Winston Churchill: "short words are best, and old words, when short, are best of all." We used this quote to introduce a leader in 2004. It went on:

> And, not for the first time, he was right: short words are best. Plain they may be, but that is their strength. They are clear, sharp and to the point. You can get your tongue round them. You can spell them. Eye, brain and mouth work as one to greet them as friends, not foes. For that is what they are. They do all that you want of them, and they do it well. On a good day, when all is right with the world, they are one more cause for cheer. On a bad day, when the head aches, you can get to grips with them, grasp their drift and take hold of what they mean. And thus they make you want to read on, not turn the page.

Sharp-eyed readers will have seen the trick: there is not a word longer than one syllable in this paragraph. And on it went like that, for the rest of the piece, 783 old, short words.

Why are old words short and best? A brief history

English is capacious, with a vocabulary rich not only in synonyms but in near-synonyms that have subtle differences. The ability to choose the right one is a hallmark of a good writer.

Some insecure writers are tempted by a thesaurus when trying to vary their vocabulary. But a good rule is that if you need a thesaurus, you have no business using one. A thesaurus can tell you that *help*, *aid*, *assist* and *support* all have similar meanings. But it can't tell you which is the right one for your sentence. You need to know both words' definitions and their connotations—the shadings that differ when you choose between *thin* and *skinny*.

Sometimes words really do mean almost the exact same thing. You would need a microscope to tease apart any difference in meaning between *get* and *obtain*. They do differ, though: in the kinds of situations in which you might use them. Try offering to *obtain someone a drink* at the next party you go to and see if they are there when you return. You *obtain a mortgage* but *get a beer*.

The reason *get* and *obtain* feel different has to do with the last 1,500 years or so of the English language. Understanding the origins of words is crucial to understanding their impact. Why does *kingly* have a fantasy-fiction feel, whereas *royal* implies a literal monarch, and *regal* is more figurative? Given a choice between rough-hewn and refined, which should you go for? Which of *rough-hewn* and *refined* feels rough-hewn, and which feels refined?

A skilled English-speaker would know the answer to that question even without ever having seen them before. And the reasons have to do with history. We speak English, not "British", for reasons to do with the conquest of the island of Great Britain by successive groups, each of which left a distinctive mark on the language that still affects how we use it today.

Britons, Anglo-Saxons and Vikings

The pre-Roman inhabitants of Great Britain, called Britons, spoke Celtic languages related to modern Welsh and Irish. They were conquered by Rome, but ordinary Britons never began speaking Latin, as their neighbours in France had. If they had, today the "British" language would be a Romance cousin to French and Spanish. Instead, the Britons kept their Celtic, and spoke it still when the Roman empire retreated in the fifth century.

But the Celtic languages of Britain did not dominate for much longer. The island tempted new invaders from southern Denmark and northern Germany: the Angles, Saxons, Jutes and others today lumped together as "Anglo-Saxons". They conquered most of Great Britain, pushing the Celtic-speakers west and north towards Wales, Cornwall and Scotland.

The Anglo-Saxon victory—in linguistic terms—was total. Today's Britons don't speak British because, after just a few centuries, the Celtic languages were restricted to the northern and western reaches of the island. Instead, we speak the language named after the Angles: Anglisc, or English, the Germanic language of the conquerors, not the Celtic of the conquered. Though conquerors and conquered usually mix their languages extensively, to this day scholars wonder why there is almost no Celtic in English. Just a few words like *dun* and *crag* are all that remain.

A few centuries later, Britain once again tempted invaders, this time the Vikings. They not only came and ransacked; many settled. Alfred the Great, the best-known of the Anglo-Saxon kings, fought them to a truce. The Vikings and Alfred divided the island. The Vikings could settle north of their line in the Danelaw, leaving the Anglo-Saxons alone south of it. (To this day, place-names with Viking elements like -*by*—think of Grimsby and Derby—are far commoner in the old Danelaw.)

The Vikings, like the people they raided, spoke a Germanic language, in their case Old Norse, a cousin to Anglo-Saxon. Vikings and Anglo-Saxons could understand each other, though with difficulty, when each spoke their own language.

Over time, Viking settlers took English wives, settled down and had English-speaking children. Naturally this led to them contributing their own words to English. These included things we might stereotypically associate with Vikings—violent words like *knife* and *ransack*. But the Vikings also contributed *window*, *leg*, *husband* and even *they*. The fact that these are everyday words shows how closely the Norse and Anglo-Saxon speakers rubbed shoulders. In some cases, Norse borrowings settled in next to Saxon words rather than displacing them, giving English quasi-synonyms like *heaven* (Anglo-Saxon) and *sky* (Norse), or *hide* (Anglo-Saxon) and *skin* (Norse).

Sometimes English imported a close cousin of a word it already had. *Ship* and *skiff* are, respectively, Anglo-Saxon and Norse pronunciations of the same Germanic word; over time the two took on distinct meanings. The same is true of *shirt* and *skirt*, and *shatter* and *scatter*. In such pairs the close kinship of the languages is clear.

Conquest and renaissance

Not so with the next invaders. In 1066 William the Conqueror came from Normandy and took the English throne. Now England was run by speakers of a northern dialect of French. For centuries, the Normans were a small minority amid the large Saxon population. The kings of England hardly spoke English.

This is why the Normans gave English words with cachet, dealing with the law (*arrest*), religion (*abbey*), warfare (*army*) and style (*art*), just to start with A. Animals and their meat have different names in English because Saxon farmers lived near their *pigs*, *sheep* and *cows* (all Germanic words), while Norman lords ate the *pork*, *mutton* and *beef* (all from French). French was the language of *royalty*—a word they also gave to English.

In continental Europe Latin was still the language of all serious writing. As a result, the long infiltration of Latin words into English began in earnest after the Norman conquest. Latin words were especially common in religion (*diocese*, *scripture*), law (*homicide*, *testify*) and learning (*history*, *library*).

The last significant source of new words came after the Renaissance. Scholars rediscovered Greek, and began not only borrowing words from Classical Greek (*chaos*, *physics*) but even coining their own new words from Greek roots (*utopia*, *zoology*), just as they had been doing with Latin roots. In this era, the prestige of English was at a low ebb. If a fancy new word was needed, one constructed from classical rather than Saxon parts would sound more impressive. In many cases, a classical coinage (like *conscience*) pushed its Saxon predecessor (*inwit*) into obsolescence. But in other cases, the new bedded in with the old, giving English elegant words from Greek or Latin alongside synonyms from Anglo-Saxon.

In the early modern period, the English (who, after the union with Scotland, began calling themselves "British") set out to conquer the world. As they did, their language was enriched by many of the languages they encountered, from Spanish (*bronco*) to Nahuatl (*chocolate*) to Hindi (*juggernaut*). These many words provide variety and richness to the language, and colonialism is often described as a major contributor to English. But in numerical terms, the words contributed by colonial contact are a small part of the total.

English is often called a "mixed" or even a "mongrel" language because of all these influences. But that obscures two fundamental points. Though the vocabulary is indeed mixed, the language itself remains that of the invaders of 500AD: a Germanic tongue. The Saxons made the Celts learn their language, not the other way round. Viking husbands learned their English wives' language, not the other way round. The Normans, after a few centuries, learned their peasants' language, not the other way round. We still speak Anglo-Saxon: not a true hybrid of Saxon, Celtic, Latin, French, Norse and Greek, but an "Englisc" enriched by these other languages.

That is why, although French and Latin sources each account for about 29% of the words in an unabridged dictionary and Greek another 6%, we don't use those words with equal frequency. *The* is used about 250,000 times as often as *exegete*. One study has found that across writings from different genres, about 49% of the words used were of Germanic origin. Just 18% came from the modern Romance languages (including French), 7% from Latin, 0.2% from Greek and 0.2% from all other languages combined.

So Anglo-Saxon words have a special status in English. They are the oldest words in the language. They are the most common. They are the most semantically basic: the first words a child learns, or the words a foreigner would need in order to survive (*help! food! water! sleep!*). Concrete nouns and vivid verbs, the subject of the next section, tend to be Germanic.

Anglo-Saxon words also have a different sound and feel from French- or Latin-derived equivalents. They are shorter, even monosyllabic. When they have multiple syllables the stress falls more often on the first, giving them a distinct rhythm. All this has a profound *psychological impression*—in Saxon, a *deep mark in the soul*— on readers.

A text that relies primarily on Germanic, Anglo-Saxon vocabulary will feel more *hearty* than *cordial*. Few readers will know why. What they are sensing is that Anglo-Saxon accounts for most of the words people use when they talk. Those from French, and even more so Latin and Greek, are those that they primarily use when they read and write.

Talking is effortless for most people; writing is difficult for most. Children speak without instruction; they are fluent before they can tie their shoelaces. The world has many illiterate peoples, but none who lacks a spoken language. Writing is hard, learned formally over many years.

A truly classic style of writing, paradoxical as it may seem, is one that feels like conversation. It is that of a good friend telling a story over coffee, rather than someone trying to impress or bewilder you in a classroom or courtroom. A classic style is warm and genuine. It draws readers in and makes them feel that they and the writer are partners.

This preference for Anglo-Saxon vocabulary is not a matter of English chauvinism. (English itself, remember, is an import to England.) But if you have the choice between an Anglo-Saxon word and its Latin or French equivalent, the former will give you a grounded and genuine feel, the latter an elevated, impersonal one. Every word in "short words are best, and old words when short are best of all" is Anglo-Saxon.

No rule should be taken to extremes. Consider "Uncleftish Beholding" by Poul Anderson, which offers Anglo-Saxon fetishism as parody: what if all the words in a scientific essay, in this case an explanation of atomic theory, were Germanic?

> The underlying kinds of stuff are the firststuffs, which link together in sundry ways to give rise to the rest. Formerly we knew of ninety-two firststuffs, from waterstuff, the lightest and barest, to ymirstuff, the heaviest. Now we have made more, such as aegirstuff and helstuff.
>
> The firststuffs have their being as motes called unclefts. These are mightly small; one seedweight of waterstuff holds a tale of them like unto two followed by twenty-two naughts. Most unclefts link together to make what are called bulkbits. Thus, the waterstuff bulkbit bestands of two waterstuff unclefts, the sourstuff bulkbit of two sourstuff unclefts, and so on.

Even more than our one-syllable leader, the results are odd. The modern sciences emerged in that early modern period during which Latin and Greek were at the height of their prestige. From *linguistics* (from Latin "lingua", tongue) to *economics* (from Greek "oikos" and "nomos", the law of running a home), even the names of the disciplines themselves are unutterable without Greek and Latin words.

The average writer is not an armchair etymologist. With a small amount of study you can begin to develop a feel for which words are Latinate and which are Germanic. But this is not the main aim of most writers. The goal is readable prose.

Fortunately, by asking yourself just a few questions about a word you can choose more of those that will give your writing a genuine, grounded feel:

Is it short?
Do I ever use it when talking to friends?
Does nearly everyone know it?
Can I recall great authors from centuries past using it?

These are signs that you have reached the bedrock of English vocabulary. You will sometimes need to use words that come from the higher, newer layers of the language. But building on a solid base that all readers know and use will mean you can do so with the greatest impact.

In each case below, for example, the first is Germanic, and almost always your better choice. Prefer:

buy to *purchase* or *acquire*	*make* to *manufacture*
let to *permit*	*set up* to *establish*
about to *approximately*	*show* to *demonstrate*
enough to *sufficient*	*spending* to *expenditure*
give to *donate*	*give up* to *relinquish*
help to *aid*	*break* to *violate*
get to *obtain*	*hand out* to *distribute*

No rule is absolute. The general rule—to use the words that ordinary people do in conversation—should override etymology. Prefer:

present (noun) to *gift* (the French-derived word is more common);
people to *persons* (both are Latinate, but the first is much more genuine);
rich to *wealthy*, but to *however*, *after* to *following* (all Germanic, but the first of each pair is sharper).

Nouns like a rock

Nouns seem to be the most fundamental words: the first words a child learns, and the first you pick up in a new language. They are indeed basic, but they are also often misunderstood.

You may have been taught that a noun is a "person, place or thing". That definition suits a young learner, for whom the easiest nouns to think of are things they can point to: a *dog* or a *house*. But it is far from complete. Is *nothingness*, for instance, a thing or the very opposite of a thing? What about *destruction*? That looks more like an action, and we tell children that verbs, not nouns, are for action. A comedian once mocked the "war on terrorism" by saying you couldn't declare war on terrorism: "It isn't even a noun!" But of course it is. What he meant is that terrorism is not one of those people-place-thing nouns that you can point at.

In fact, nouns are defined by grammatical properties, not physical ones. Simply stated, nouns are the words that perform certain roles in sentences. (Nouns are the words that do nouny things.) They can, for example, be the subject of a sentence. Now you can see that the examples above are nouns: *Nothingness* is a terrifying concept. The *destruction* of the village was imminent. They can be direct objects, often receiving the action of the verb, as in *He saw the destruction of the village.* They can be possessive (*The destruction's impact is still being felt today.*) None of these things can be done by, say, a preposition.

But though nouns are not "things", things are still important. Identifiable, visible people, places and things that you can point to are a special kind of noun: the concrete kind. Concrete nouns are not always objects you can stub your toe on—try stubbing your toe on the *wind* or the *coronasphere*—but it can help to think of them that way.

Above all, concrete nouns are things that actually exist in the world and, as such, they are the object of vivid writing. People and the things they do. Objects and how they behave. In science, the relevant concrete nouns might be matter: elements, or animals, or planets. In business, nouns might be products, customers, workers or shops.

Concrete nouns can also be described in terms of their opposites: abstract nouns. These words describe concepts, ones you will never stub your toe on. Some abstract nouns are beautiful: *love*, *time*, *language*. But far too many of them are the bane of good writing.

Among them are *nominalisations*, boring nouns made from verbs, like *observation* from *observe*. *Nominalisation* is, of course, itself a nominalisation. One writer, Helen Sword of the University of Auckland, calls them "zombie nouns" for their habit of stalking lifeless through prose.

For example, if we want to relate the number of people seeking work, we describe the *unemployment rate*. What is a *rate*? It isn't a thing, but an observation about the amount of something else (*unemployment*). We can take this one step further if, for example, we discuss a *rise in the unemployment rate*. If we see things that make us worry that such a rise is on the horizon, we might go on: *leading indicators of a rise in the unemployment rate*. And so on.

Words for concepts (like *unemployment*) have their uses, of course. Economists need abstractions. But underneath the dry *unemployment level* are millions of living human stories of frustration, even despair: people fruitlessly leafing through job ads day after day, worrying about how they are going to feed their families. It is more efficient for economists, and perhaps also more comfortable for politicians, to talk about the "unemployment level". But it is often best, even if painful, to use concrete words, about *people seeking work and unable to find it*.

Academic, bureaucratic and related kinds of writing can seem to be written as though there are no humans or tangible objects in the world they are describing. Instead the world is filled with *levels, observations, phenomena, manifestations, instances, indications, predictions*. Take this recent summary of an academic study, on an exciting topic, and note how the writer has desiccated it with his choice of nouns (all of which are in italics).

> This *paper* examines the *impact* of *cell phone access* on *election fraud*. I combine *cell phone coverage maps* with the *location* of *polling centers* during the 2009 Afghan presidential *election* to pinpoint which *centers* were exposed to *coverage*. Results from a spatial *regression discontinuity design* along the two-dimensional *coverage boundary* suggest that *coverage* deters corrupt *behaviour*.

The nouns are dominated by abstraction: *impact, access, coverage, location, results, regression, discontinuity, design, boundary* and *behaviour*. The other nouns are more promising: *fraud, cell phone, polling centre, election*. Not all of these are concrete, but even the abstractions (*fraud, election*) are more vivid. As they should be: the paper finds that the more cell-phone towers an area had, the fewer illegal votes were stuffed into ballot boxes. An interesting topic, and one worthy of clear description.

Concrete nouns are the kind that you can picture in the mind's eye. And that eye is more than a metaphor. The eyes merely receive light, but the brain processes it and makes sense of it. Researchers have found that concrete nouns stimulate brain regions that abstract ones do not. There really is something special about people, places and things.

When you stimulate not only the language circuitry but also the visual circuitry, you are giving your readers two mutually reinforcing ways of dealing with information. The words provoke the images in the mind; the images in turn reinforce the understanding of the words, in a virtuous cycle. (Memorable sounds, rather than images, can offer a similar benefit. They stimulate the brain's auditory circuitry, which is why rhythm and rhyme also make words more memorable.)

So concrete nouns make life easier for your readers, who can "see" what you are talking about as well as think about it. And *cognitive ease is highly associated with perceptions of persuasiveness*. Or, as ordinary human beings would say it: *people like and trust things they can easily understand*.

A final, compelling reason to use concrete nouns when you write is to keep yourself focused on what you are actually writing about. Readers don't care about levels or phenomena or observations. This is why journalists often begin articles with a vignette, a named person in a predicament, before going on to describe the forces (unemployment, lack of education) that landed them there. Readers might not care that *The rise in salaries is not commensurate with consumer-price inflation*, but might be more moved by *Grocery bills are growing faster than pay packets*.

Sometimes an abstract word is the most strictly accurate one. But vivid writing often relies on a reader's common sense to fill in the picture. So see if you can replace:

workforce with *workers*
compensation with *pay*

revenue with *sales*
high-net-worth individuals with *rich people*
inventory with *goods, stocks, products on shelves*
civil society with NGOS (or perhaps *community organisations*)
conflict with *fighting* or *war*
the intelligence community with *spies*
academic community with *scholars*
the international community with nearly anything more accurate.

Verbs that do something

Just as a noun is inaccurately defined as a "person, place or thing", a verb is often called an "action word". This, too, is incomplete. Many of the things people "do" are distinctly inactive (*rest, sleep, dawdle, hesitate*). But many verbs don't involve a living thing doing anything at all, even resting. What kind of action is involved in the verbs *be, remain, exist* or *seem*?

Verbs, like nouns, are defined by the part they play in sentences. That is, they are where the action is, metaphysically if not literally. In a declarative sentence—a statement about something—the verb is where the declaration itself hinges. Cats *chase* mice (a description of action) or Ouagadougou *is* the capital of Burkina Faso (a comment on Ouagadougou).

Verbs are therefore supremely important, and too often neglected. The problem often begins with abstract nouns. Prose heavy with ponderous nouns also tends to feature empty verbs. It is as though the writer hopes that the noun, or perhaps a ponderous noun phrase (the noun and all its attendant baggage), will do the talking.

This leaves the verb as practically an afterthought. Looking again at the academic abstract above, you will see a positively lumbering noun phrase: "Results from a spatial regression discontinuity design along the two-dimensional coverage boundary". This is our subject; the verb is going to tell us something about it. But what do these results do? They "suggest". This sentence is the crux of the paper, encapsulating what the ingenious scholar discovered about mobile phones, voters and fraud. But we have a lifeless entity ("results") doing a lifeless thing ("suggesting"). The first few sentences of the paper go on in the same way: "developing countries have experienced";

"a growing literature has shown" but "our understanding has not moved."

The thread linking all these sentences is the pairing of abstract nouns with empty verbs. They seem to attract each other like particles with an opposite charge. Meanwhile, consider concrete nouns and the kind of verbs they attract. Citizens *vote* for a candidate. Malefactors *stuff* ballot-boxes. Observers *share* information, with their phones, about what they have seen. These are not particularly action-packed verbs, but all call a visual image to mind: the voter putting a ballot into a box, the concerned observer placing a call, and so on. Concrete nouns seem naturally to do real things you can picture. It is in their nature to attract vivid verbs.

Especially lively verbs have another quality: they save the need for extra words by packing in meaning, telling the reader not only what was done but how. Many writing guides teach "write with nouns and verbs, not adjectives and adverbs." What they mean is that a more specific noun or verb often allows you to dispense with adjectives and adverbs entirely. Consider the difference between *walk* and *strut*, or *say* and *murmur*. The latter of each pair is not only a little more interesting; it carries more information, and so is more efficient. You could write *walk proudly* or *say softly*, but these are flabbier options. Make your verbs strut.

If you are talking about identifiable people, objects and actions, you are not only less likely to trip over your language. You are also less likely to make obvious logical flaws or other errors, because your tangible subjects are clear in the mind. If they do something implausible or illogical in your writing, you will see it.

By contrast, when the people and things disappear in a blizzard of abstraction, it is much easier to lose track of what you hope to say. The process becomes a defensive one of stitching sentences together and hoping that nothing goes wrong, rather than an active one of saying cleanly what you mean.

But the most important benefit of writing with tangible nouns and vivid verbs comes not while you are typing, but when your reader starts reading. A reader's mind begins to engage when a thread of meaning emerges from a piece of writing. Protagonists, antagonists, a challenge, a resolution: the same things that make for a good story can also drive a piece of analysis. Your reader is more likely not only to finish what you write, but to remember it—and maybe even act on it.

Replace:

demonstrates an unwillingness to with *refuses to*
manifests avoidance behaviour with *avoids*
the proliferation of abstractions exhibits a deadening tendency upon writing with *empty words deaden writing*

Euphemism and exaggeration

When writing about difficult subjects—war, inequality, crime, discrimination, corruption, etc—there are two dangers. One is weakening, often through abstraction: *abuses of power* instead of clearer descriptions like *fraud* or *bribery*.

Making sure that you are still accurate, aim to replace:

homelessness with *people sleeping rough*
human-rights abuses with *torture, murder, massacres*, etc
civilian casualties or *collateral damage* with *dead civilians*
mortality with *death*
voting irregularities with *vote-rigging*
redundancies with *lay-offs*
the underprivileged with *poor people, people struggling to pay the bills*, etc
sexual assault with *rape, groping*, etc
kinetic action with *battle*

The other danger, however, is the temptation to exaggerate, reaching for more explosive words than are warranted. Not every problem is a *crisis*, nor is every allegation of wrongdoing a *scandal*. Not every important event needs to be dignified as *historic*, and not all political speech as *rhetoric* (if only). Such words lose their force by over-use: what will you call a real crisis when one arrives?

Being accurate—neither too vague nor too emotive—is not only an ethical and legal imperative. It also builds credibility by demonstrating a willingness to describe things fairly, as they really are.

The use and abuse of jargon

Professional jargon has a technical function. You can't be a doctor if you don't know the names of the parts of the body, or of the processes and diseases it undergoes. But learning the jargon is not only a way to master knowledge. It is also a way to show off—both to people inside the group (fellow doctors) and to those outside it (patients).

Take *hyperemesis gravidarum*, a serious condition suffered by some pregnant women. An obstetrician will explain that it involves serious nausea and uncontrolled vomiting. And the label of the disease gives the doctor's diagnosis an air of learning. But a classicist might scoff: "hyper" merely means "super" or "a lot", in Greek. And "emesis" means nothing more than "vomit". Finally "gravidarum" is Latin for "of pregnancy". If you tell your doctor "I'm pregnant and throwing up all the time," and your doctor replies "You have what is technically known as 'pregnancy supervomit'," you will not be impressed.

Such terminology puts a distance between doctor and patient, and may make the patient feel alienated from her condition and treatment. A good doctor will explain conditions like hyperemesis well. But in the main, doctors are trained to treat those conditions, and not to translate all that Greek for the patient. Your job as a writer, on the other hand, is precisely that: translation, or explanation.

Translation is even more important when politicians or businesses try to bury bad news, put a shine on mediocre ideas or generally try to sound impressive by using terms beloved of insiders yet never once heard in casual conversation. Avoid the following pitfalls:

1. Pomposity. *Meetings* or *conferences* are dressed up as *summits*. *Granular* is edging out *detailed*. *Brainstorming* has become *ideation*, and at one of those ideation sessions it was decided that *learnings* were more valuable than *lessons* and *optics* classier than *appearances*. None of these improves on the older, more common word; nothing has been added except novelty.

2. Verbing. There is nothing inherently wrong with verbs formed from nouns. English is full them. Shakespeare was a master verber (*Grace me no grace, nor uncle me no uncle*). Some verbed nouns settle into the language over time: *contact* and *host* were considered horrible as verbs not long ago.

But unless you are Shakespeare you are more likely to annoy than entertain with novel verbings. It may be only a matter of time before no one is bothered by *to impact* or *to access*, but they still annoy enough readers that you should write *to have an impact on* or *to gain access to*. Similarly, find alternatives for *to showcase*, to *source*, to *segue* and to *target*. Newer verbings are even more noxious to readers: the likes of to *action*, to *gift*, to *interface* and to *whiteboard* should never escape the office meeting-room.

3. Misdirection. Many jargon words seem designed to obscure. When companies merge, they inevitably promise *synergy*—that the two partners can do more together than apart. Scratch the surface and this usually means that they can do more with fewer workers.

But then matters take their course. The company detects *issues* (never "problems"). These might entail a *cyclical downturn* (a *recession*, so nobody is buying their product at the moment) or a *secular downturn* (which means that *their industry is shrinking*, and people won't buy the product tomorrow, either). Soon begins the talk of *reallocation of resources*, *refocusing*, *downsizing* (even *rightsizing*) and so on. Call these things what they are.

When and how to use specialist terms

Most writers, especially in business, finance, economics and science, will need to use specialised words on occasion. You should first identify those terms you will re-use often enough in your writing that they are worth keeping. They are best, in effect, taught to your reader. Explaining an unfamiliar concept in terms of a familiar one (a metaphor) is an effective way to do this (see next chapter).

The terms you need to define may be fewer than you think. Some examples from grammar show how you can phrase a term of art in words that everyone knows. *Syntax*, for example, is how words are combined into bigger units like phrases, clauses and sentences. If you don't plan to linger on syntax, you don't need to use it at all: you can simply talk about *how words are combined*. An even rarer term for a common thing is *morphology*: putting words and bits of words together to make longer words, like the three pieces of "un-lady-like".

Linguists love morphology, but when talking to wider audiences they're better served by talking about *building words out of smaller pieces*. When you will not be re-using terms frequently, rephrasing is your best strategy.

Acronyms and initialisms are common in technical writing, but they are wearying to a reader who is not familiar with them, and deadening even to one who is. You may think that, having defined "hyperemesis gravidarum" once, you can simply go on to refer to HG throughout your writing. But this forces the reader to recall the unfamiliar phrase behind the initials; it saves you a few keystrokes at the expense of the reader's ease.

Instead, consider short forms and simple synonyms. Hyperemesis gravidarum can be *the condition* on later mentions, or something general like *nausea* where precision is not crucial. A bit of work to vary your vocabulary, rather than monotonously repeating strings of capital letters, will do wonders for keeping your reader's attention.

The basket of deplorables

A full account of every word that annoys somebody—or even just one of the editors at *The Economist*—would be too long to read, and impossible to commit to memory. Instead, remember that your goal is to avoid words that are vogueish, self-important, vague or misleading.

At the time of writing, here are a few words to steer clear of:

address (as a transitive verb; try *deal with, attend to*)
aspirational
facilitate
famously (if it's famous, do you need to say so?)
high-profile
iconic
individual (as a synonym for *person*, unless there is no alternative)
inform (as a pretentious verb meaning to *influence*)
implode (since nature abhors a vacuum, few things actually implode)
key (as an adjective; especially *key players*, and do not say *this decision is key*)
major (try cutting it and seeing if context does the job instead)

move (as a synonym for *decision, policy* or *change: The move served to highlight...*)

narrative

paradigm

participate in (try *take part in*)

passionate

proactive

players (unless in sports and games)

prestigious (this means the author likes it)

reputational

savvy

segue

showcase (verb)

source (verb)

spikes (many rises so described turn out to have no descents)

stakeholders

supportive (try *helpful*)

surreal

trajectory (long word for *course* or *path*)

transformative

trigger (as a verb. Try *cause, lead to, result in*, etc.)

vision

wannabes

This list will always be changing. The words in question are used because writers think them snappy and stylish, a category that gains and loses members daily. The subheading of this section made sense in 2016, when Hillary Clinton used it on the campaign trail. One day it will be outmoded, or even unknown. A rule of thumb: was this word used two decades ago, and will it still be used that way two decades from now? If not, consider an alternative.

2

Putting words to work: phrasing, images, metaphors and style

In recent years researchers in artificial intelligence have unveiled systems that seem to "write" without any human involvement. The best of these churn out remarkably convincing prose. It can take quite a while—as long as a few paragraphs—before a reader realises that what such machines "write" doesn't always seem to cohere: that ideas don't follow logically and arguments don't make sense.

Machine-learning systems are trained on data. Feed them years of articles from, say, a newspaper and they detect patterns in the combinations of words that tend to appear. Train two identical systems, one on the *New Yorker*, say, and the other on *The Economist* (both experiments have, in fact, been tried) and the machines will churn out prose that distinctly resembles the styles of the two publications.

Before you are tempted to scoff, here is a disquieting thought: human writers are not so different from machine-learning systems. Writing may seem to be the ultimate creative act. But every time you put fingers to keyboard, you too have been "trained": by everything you have ever read, influencing subtly or unsubtly what you write.

To be influenced by other writers is inevitable and even a good thing. But many writers go beyond being influenced. They write on automatic pilot, in a style that imitates the kind of writing they read most often. The result is at best unoriginal. At worst, it is thoughtless, even meaningless.

Your aim as a writer should not only be to avoid mistakes by keeping your prose safe. You are also seeking to grab your readers' attention and, with luck, even influence them. The first step is necessary for the second—and to succeed, your language will need to be original and fresh.

The last chapter looked at pretentious words like *learnings* in place of *lessons*. But equally pervasive are longer figures of speech: the worn-out idioms and metaphors that are all too common in meeting-rooms. *Blue-sky thinking* or *thinking out of the box* for creativity. *Going forward* and *at the end of the day* to link ideas in a loose way. *The elephant in the room* or, elsewhere in the zoo, the *800-pound gorilla* or simply *big beast* to describe office personalities and dramas. *Low-hanging fruit* and *quick wins* for short-term goals. *Let's take this offline, put a pin in it* or *put it in the parking lot* for *let's talk about this later*, and *reach out* or *circle back* for communication plans.

Some of these clichés are already old enough to have been mocked into obsolescence. But the stock of catchphrases is constantly being refreshed. Here are some examples of business jargon noted down by a long-suffering correspondent at *The Economist* who was sent on a management-training course:

Chunking up to a meta-level
The other side of the visionary coin
Taking up some of that limited bandwidth fruitfully
When we're joining the dots we want to be walking the walk
From soup to nuts across our organisation and beyond
We can suck it and see, let a thousand flowers bloom, water our strategic shoots
One of the thrust-lines we like to look down when decision-making

When first coined, new expressions by definition cannot be clichés. Perhaps they are even witty. For a while they are limited to a small circle: if you're the first one to use a new phrase, you may seem (in another cliché) ahead of the curve. It won't last. Clichés are like invasive species, quickly taking over if not ruthlessly culled.

While each generation's tropes are new, the problem isn't. Every age has clichés, and writing commentators to bemoan them. But Orwell went beyond complaining, to do some analysis. He distinguished usefully between figures of speech that were "dead" and those that were "dying".

The "dead" group, he thought, were not a problem. They have become so common that they barely evoke the original referent: *iron will*, his example, no longer calls to mind images of the grey metal.

Orwell's real target was the figures of speech that have enough life left in them to make writers and speakers think they are more vivid than they are. Here are his examples:

> Ring the changes on, take up the cudgels for, toe the line, ride roughshod over, stand shoulder to shoulder with, play into the hands of, no axe to grind, grist to the mill, fishing in troubled waters, on the order of the day, Achilles' heel, swan song, hotbed.

The problem with such ready-made phrases, he argued, is that they can be strung together without conscious effort. This saves the writer the work of first thinking of what to say, and then saying it with the most effective possible language.

But writing afresh, though more difficult, is worth the effort. Original imagery seizes your reader's imagination. The first person to say *the elephant in the room* undoubtedly made listeners picture an awkwardly placed pachyderm. Today, it evokes nothing much. You must come up with a new elephant.

Consider another image, again from Orwell, describing someone spouting predictable propaganda:

> One often has a curious feeling that one is not watching a live human being but some kind of dummy: a feeling which suddenly becomes stronger at moments when the light catches the speaker's spectacles and turns them into blank discs which seem to have no eyes behind them.

You probably involuntarily pictured what Orwell was talking about. He could have stopped at describing the man as a *dummy* (today we would say a *puppet*), but this would have left little impression. Instead the extra effort made, to give the striking detail of the light on the spectacles, leaves an impression that lasts even after you have finished the essay. Fresh imagery is effective because it gives the reader two ways to process what you are saying: one logical and linguistic, and another visual.

Indeed, his essay on the dangers of hackneyed language is full of striking images:

The writer knows more or less what he wants to say, but an accumulation of stale phrases chokes him *like tea-leaves blocking a sink.*

If the speech he is making is one that he is accustomed to make over and over again, he may be almost unconscious of what he is saying, *as one is when one utters the responses in church.*

When there is a gap between one's real and one's declared aims, one turns as it were instinctively to long words and exhausted idioms, *like a cuttlefish spurting out ink.*

Phrases like *a not unjustifiable assumption, leaves much to be desired, would serve no good purpose, a consideration which we should do well to bear in mind* are a continuous temptation, *a packet of aspirins always at one's elbow.*

Coming up with fresh phrasings like these takes effort and time. But the effort, and whatever time you have available, are well worth it. Try to replace the phrases below with something fresher:

accident waiting to happen
chattering classes
deer in the headlights
eye-watering sums
fit for purpose
game-changer
going forward (in the sense of in future)
the green light
grinding to a halt
heavy lifting
honeymoon period

level playing-field
paradigm shift
perfect storm
poster child
pulling teeth
rack up (profits, etc)
ramping up
tipping point
too close to call
wake-up call
whopping bills

Journalese

Alongside clichés proper, the special idiom of journalism deserves special mention. Here is a representative newspaper story:

RUSSIA *RATCHETS UP PRESSURE* ON EUROPE, SAYS 'NO GROUNDS' FOR FURTHER TALKS ON SECURITY AMID *HEIGHTENED TENSIONS*

A top Russian official said there were "no grounds" to
continue security talks to *defuse* the crisis over Ukraine's aim
to join NATO — a rebuff to the West as part of a *hardline blitz* by
Moscow envoys Thursday that ended in an *impasse* after days of
high-stakes diplomacy.

The remarks by the Russian Deputy Foreign Minister *amped
up the pressure* on the Biden administration and its allies as they
struggle to *find a path out from tensions* between NATO and Russia
and avert a potential new war in Europe.

This week's *flurry* of meetings in Europe was seen as a *critical
bid* by the United States and NATO partners amid fears Russia
could launch a *multipronged attack* on Ukraine — a former Soviet
republic whose government has *built ties* with the West, but is
seen by Moscow as part of its *sphere of influence*....

The phrasing is typical of geopolitical writing: *ratchets, pressure,
tension, defusing,* a *blitz,* an *impasse, high stakes, amping up, flurries,
bids, ties, spheres.* In three short paragraphs, the writer deploys
metaphors to do with machinery, physics, bomb-making, warfare,
gambling, audio technology, weather and geometry. An uncharitable
evaluation is that this is fatally mangled.

The more charitable, and realistic, explanation is that all of these
metaphors are, in Orwell's terms, not dying but dead. In this view,
nobody imagines physical *pressure* any more in this context, and
so don't mind such pressure being increased by *amping up,* as one
originally did a guitar. And while guitar strings might be under literal
tension, the word is now so common in political writing that readers
don't mind when they are *heightened* (or *boiling, simmering, inflamed*
or *defused,* as they so often are).

But this defence is hardly a ringing one. It is to say that the writer
has relied on images so commonplace that they no longer have any
impact on the reader whatsoever. For the reader to whom the dying
metaphors still have meaning, the text is erratic and confusing. To
those to whom the images are dead, it will have a narcotic effect.

In the prose of journalists on deadline all lawns are *manicured*
with a *white picket fence,* all conservative towns in the American South
are the *buckle of the Bible belt,* all oil-rich countries have a *long-serving
strongman.* Clever politicians come in two varieties, the *policy wonk*

and the *wily political operator*, who will invariably wind up involved in a scandal dubbed something-*gate*. Political decisions are *watershed*, *landmark* or *sea-change* moments. All negotiations are *11th-hour*, *marathon, make-or-break*. The journalist, of course, knows all this after talking to *key players*, perhaps *well-placed insiders*.

Structural elements also come in over-used, ready-made varieties: the rubric that reads "*A is trying to do B. It will not be easy.*" The weary opening of the journalist who has seen it all: *another week, another X*. The introduction of a bit of hopeful novelty: *first the good news*. Then the turn: *now for the bad news*. Summing up, the news given in the story is put in context: it is no *silver bullet* or *panacea* (which really would be news). But *one thing is for certain*...

Metaphor magic

One way to know that a writer has not really thought carefully before choosing metaphors is that they come in humorous, clashing proximity to each other. Mashed-up metaphors are particularly common in business-speak. By no means let phrases like this pass through your fingers, and do not quote an executive saying them unless you intend to make them look silly.

> We're in the *early innings* of this *sea change*.
> It is a *wake-up call* to the people who thought that the crisis was just a *flesh wound*.
> Share buybacks' *momentum* is finally *cooling down*.
> Our company is continually *tailoring* its products to customers' constantly evolving *palates*.
> The next generation of business leaders is *bubbling under the radar*.
> The new product *roadmap* has hit some *turbulence*.

But lack of care for metaphors is doubly a shame because when done well they are a powerful device. Think about the scientific metaphors that make sense of otherwise baffling phenomena: the atom as a solar system, or gravity distorting space-time like a bowling ball on a rubber sheet.

Sometimes a metaphor is an aid to your own thinking. Darwin was inspired by the discovery that languages changed extremely slowly, but that given enough time, two forms of speech can become mutually unintelligible. It helped him develop the idea that species evolved and diverged a bit like that too.

When you write with metaphors, the important thing is to be consistent and intentional. It can sometimes be a good idea to develop one over the course of an entire piece, whether you are explaining a complicated issue (the blockchain is something like a ledger) or making a light-hearted comparison (the political leader as symphony conductor, or master chef). You might introduce this metaphor early on, refer to it throughout and neatly tie it up in your closing sentences—though like a master chef, be careful not to overdo it with a single ingredient.

Metaphors can also be a valuable aid to argumentation in opinion writing. An apt comparison can help you make your case. Even if it were true that climate change has only a small chance of being catastrophic, the catastrophe would be so great that it is worth taking out insurance (as many people do for fires in their home) or making lifestyle changes (as people sensibly do when told they have a 10% risk of a heart attack in the next decade). The point of the analogy here is to show them that they already insure against other things that may not happen—but will be terrible if they do.

Metaphors by their nature are not the thing they are being compared to. You risk your argument if you use a metaphor and then expert (or merely picky) readers notice fundamental differences between the two things being compared. This is another reason, besides stylistic appeal, to choose carefully.

But smaller differences between the two things being compared can be tolerated. The blockchain is like a ledger, but is distributed across vast numbers of users, unlike a ledger-book in a shop. Languages change incrementally, but unfortunate changes do not lead to the deaths of their speakers. It can be a good idea to anticipate places where your metaphor does not line up, and explain why.

Borrowing specialist terms

Be careful with words and phrases chosen from a technical field. They do not always mean to specialists what they are loosely used by journalists to mean. A *crescendo* in music is a passage of increasing volume (it means "growing" in Italian), not the point of peak volume.

An *epicentre* is not the heart of an earthquake, but the spot on the Earth's surface above it (from *epi-*, Greek for "upon"). A hurricane is calm, not most intense, at the *eye of the storm*. *Calculus* deals with limits, and differentiation and integration of functions; for example, how position, velocity and acceleration are related. For those who know it, it is not just a fancy synonym for *calculation*, political or otherwise.

Words frequently pass from technical meanings to different non-technical ones (*squaring the circle* was once a byword for a mathematical impossibility, but this has come to refer to ordinary, if difficult, tasks). And words may abandon their etymological roots. (*Crescent* and *croissant* share an origin with *crescendo*, but refer to the shape of a growing moon.)

But in cases where the technical meanings are alive and well, available in any pocket dictionary, hazy usage will distract readers familiar with the precise ones. Watch out for:

quantum leap: not a big one. The idiom arises from physics, where the quanta involved are fixed multiples of a minuscule amount of energy. Use to describe a sudden change without intermediate stages, not a vast leap.

begging the question: this phrase originated in classical philosophy, meaning to try to smuggle the conclusion you are trying to argue into an assumption. If someone says *Illegal immigrants must be deported because they have broken the law*, they are presupposing (or avoiding arguing) that the law is just or wise, and so begging the question. But if you merely mean that something *raises* or *prompts the question*, say that.

parsing: in grammar, this means noting the details of function and form of the words in a sentence. Avoid using it as a fancy synonym for *examining*.

exponential growth: not just any rapid growth, but the kind implied by $2^1, 2^2, 2^3, 2^4, 2^5, 2^6$, or $2, 4, 8, 16, 32, 64$.

inflection point: borrowed from calculus to describe a point where a curve's concavity changes. This should not be used to indicate a mere change in direction.

marginal: poor-quality land at the edge of a field brought into cultivation is marginal. The cost of producing just one more widget in your factory is the *marginal cost of production*. The decreasing level of happiness you gain from making progressively more money is *diminishing marginal utility*. These are interesting and precise uses of *marginal*. As a synonym for *slight* or *small*, it is of marginal usefulness.

Variation, elegant and inelegant

Synonyms can enhance your writing. They can help you avoid baffling readers with technical vocabulary, and boring them by repeating everyday words. Taken too far, however, the search for what is known as "elegant variation" can get silly. Newspapers sometimes like to tickle their readers by referring to cucumbers on second mention as *the cylindrical salad-topper* or Jersey potatoes as *the smooth springtime spuds*. Avoid this temptation.

Filling a page with capital letters to avoid repetition is also ugly. The International Monetary Fund can be the IMF on occasion, and the European Central Bank the ECB. But they can also be *the fund* and *the bank*. Especially when the initialism is not well known, use such transparent phrasings so that the reader immediately knows what you are referring back to.

No originality please, we're on deadline

Under time pressure, it can be hard to come up with original headlines, captions, sub-headings and the like. Into the tired brain rushes a film, song or television reference that is put on the page as a placeholder until a better joke comes up. And it never does, leading to a profusion of half-considered pop-culture references in our pages.

So before you try it, stop and think how many times long-suffering Argentines have read *Don't cry for...* or something to do with *tango* in any story about them. Ditto *Southern discomfort* for the Americans below the Mason-Dixon line, or *Could do better* for anything about education. Or *Vive la différence* for anything about France. Or *Rise of the machines* for anything being automated. Or *mind the gap* for anything about anything: *The Economist* has used this headline at least 21 times.

The Economist has raided the name of the show "No Sex Please,

We're British" endlessly (or 23 times at least): *No sex please, we're American* (twice), *No sex please, we're Millennials; No text please, we're American; No shooting please, we're German; No gold please, we're Romanian* and even *No swots please, we're Masai.* That is probably enough.

Redundancy

Many words add nothing but length, and space is at a premium not only in the columns of a printed publication, but in your readers' minds. So cut all the cuttables that you can—it may even free up space for you to include a bit of colour or a detail that did not fit in your first draft.

Consider all of the words implied by context. *Now, currently, at present, ongoing, today* and the like are all suggested by present-tense verbs. Use these only when contrasting with another time period (*In the past... but now...*).

Try to cut *real* (*they felt real despair, wondering if real prosperity would arrive*) unless you mean taking inflation into account (*real incomes fell last year*).

Sentences with *there is/are* are best reworded. *There are three issues facing the country* is better as *The country faces three issues.*

If someone *has the ability to* do this or *the skills* to do that, try *can.*

Many redundancies also commit the crime of being clichés or journalese. The common phrases listed below are all too long, and some are dispensable entirely:

> *absolute certainty* (*certainty*)
> *pilotless drone* (*drone*)
> *razed to the ground* (*razed*)
> *track record* (*record*)
> *wilderness area* (*wilderness*)
> *policymaking process* (*policymaking*)
> *large-scale* (*large* or just *big*)
> *weather conditions* (*weather*)
> *bought up* (*bought*)
> *sold off* (*sold*)
> *headed up by* (*headed by*)

cut back, v (*cut*)
cutbacks, n (*cuts*)
end result (*result*)
for free (*free*)
from whence (*whence*)
final outcome (*outcome*)
nod your head (*nod*)
shrug your shoulders (*shrug*)
top priority (*priority*)
so-called "something" (use either quotation marks or *so-called*, not
    both)
major speech (nearly always just a *speech*)
role model (*model*)
past experience (*experience*)
lived experience (*experience*)
personal experience (*experience*)
empirical research (*research*, or *a study*)
safe haven (*haven*)
the fact that (*that* wherever possible, which is not always)
the industrial, agricultural or services sector (*industry, agriculture,*
    services)
located in (*in*)
pre-prepared (*prepared*; the *pre-* is right there already)
pre-planned (*planned*)
in close proximity to (*close to*)

Respect and clarity

There are simple ways to show respect for the people you are writing
about that do not affect the sharpness of our writing. Foremost is
to write with thoughtfulness. If you were a member of the group
described, would you feel treated with dignity, and with due respect
for the complexity involved? If your work meets this test, you may
also use plain English, and not the latest terminology favoured by
academics and activists. Your first duty is the truth.

For example, periodic efforts arise to talk about *enslaved people*
and *people experiencing homelessness* rather than *slaves* or *homeless*
people. These linguistic pushes are meant to make readers reconsider

the people being described and highlight their plight. But before long, the stigma attached to the old term attaches to the new one (*homeless people* were once called *tramps, vagrants, beggars* or *bums*). If the world around them doesn't change, the stigma around *vagrant* soon attaches to *homeless person* until it too is pejorative. Renaming the group involved does little. Good writing about their lives, using ordinary language, does more to help than linguistic reshuffling does.

That said, there are easy steps to recognise people as human beings instead of lumping them into a mass. Using nouns like *blacks, gays, Jews* or *the disabled* defines people solely by these words, as though that is all there is to them. It is better to use adjectives that modify a noun: *black leaders, gay activists, Jewish voters, disabled veterans*.

The word *community* (see also p. 95), often paired with such adjectives, is usually best replaced with another word. There are few things all members of the *Asian community* or *LGBT+ community* unanimously agree on. If you mean *organisations* or *activists*, say that.

A *poor* person has no more money, opportunity or dignity when described as *deprived, disadvantaged* or *underprivileged*. Indeed, the last of these is incoherent: if everyone has a *privilege* it is not a privilege at all. The same applies to *underdeveloped* or *developing* countries: many are not in fact developing nearly enough, and are more effectively described as *poor*.

Blind and *deaf* people refer to themselves with these common words; prefer them to *visually impaired* and *hearing impaired*. But the rules above regarding adjectives over nouns apply here too: *those with schizophrenia* rather than *schizophrenics*. *Wheelchair user* is better than *wheelchair-bound*. Unless you know that someone *suffers from* a condition (eg, because they told you), better to say that they simply *have* it. In any case, think twice about whether any disability is part of your story; if it isn't, leave it out.

This chapter has dealt with how to think about phrasings, including many examples of what you should be trying to do and what to avoid. It has not dealt with every individual issue—for anything you are still in doubt about, see Part 2, especially Chapter 6. But remember that at every step, in each sentence, you want your readers to think. Overfamiliar phrasings, to re-work a cliché, go in one eye and out the other, barely stopping at the brain. Express your ideas so that they stick.

3
Keeping it together: grammar

Most people associate "grammar" with a zealous teacher who covered school essays with red ink. Don't start a sentence with "and". Don't split an infinitive. Don't end a sentence with a preposition. The impression is of a list of "don'ts" and "nevers", one so long that no one could remember it all. This leads many people to think that they have bad grammar.

But you already know most of the grammar you need. Children in their second year begin combining nouns and verbs ("*Doggy eat*"). Soon they are constructing grammatical whole sentences. By their third year, they make increasingly complex ones with constructions such as relative clauses ("that tiger *that daddy bought*"). By school age, they are chatterboxes ready to start putting their words onto the page.

This is where the problems begin. Reading and writing are artificial, and acquired with difficulty. Even many intelligent people struggle. That is partly because written sentences are longer and more complex, and the style calls for formal tools that many people don't master. As a result, people are turned off by the very idea of grammar.

But grammar is a toolbox for building sentences up, not a schedule of rules for tearing them down. This chapter will introduce some principles for doing so effectively, before going on to some of the thorny issues that give even experienced writers trouble.

(For terminology, see the glossary on pp. 217-19.)

Keep it short

Call me Ishmael. It was the best of times; it was the worst of times. Maman died today. If you can quote the first line of a novel, there's a good chance it's one of these. Stop and think for a second what these (from "Moby Dick", "A Tale of Two Cities" and "The Stranger") have in common.

Now consider another famous opening line: *It is a truth universally acknowledged, that a single man in possession of a good fortune, must be in want of a wife.* Or this one: *Many years later, as he faced the firing squad, Colonel Aureliano Buendía was to remember that distant afternoon when his father took him to discover ice.* Elegant, to be sure. But much harder to recite from memory.

The key is concision. Short sentences are crucial to memorable writing, for the simple reason that memory is limited. This is particularly true for working memory, the kind that stores material temporarily. Remembering a ten-digit phone number is far harder than remembering a six-digit one.

When you read, you take in a stream of words, group them into grammatical chunks, and process those chunks' relationship to each other. When a chunk is incomplete—a subject has been named, say, but then a lot of words come before the verb—working memory becomes strained. (Imagine remembering a phone number while also taking your friends' drinks orders at the bar.) When the verb finally arrives, the working memory can relax. The meaning, now understood, can be stored. The exact words are no longer important, and can be forgotten. Then another sentence begins.

Reading is a constant mental workout—one you should make as easy for your readers as you can. You are also conveying information that taxes other parts of your reader's mind. By straining working memory, tricky grammar adds an extra load on top of an already difficult task. Imagine you are at the gym, performing a high-intensity series of complex exercises: squats, press-ups, sprints and so on. You wouldn't be pleased to have to don a weighted vest. This is how complex sentences feel to readers who are already working to the utmost to follow your argument.

Fortunately, there is a solution. The full stop is the writer's best friend. Frequent resort to this humble dot has two good effects. For the writer, it reduces the chances of getting tangled in syntax. Many grammar mistakes are born of long sentences with parts that stand in unclear relationship to each other. When you keep it short, you keep it simple.

For your readers, meanwhile, each full stop is a chance to clear the working memory and start over. That, in turn, makes it easier for them to focus on your argument, just as gym-goers can push themselves harder if they take short breaks. Each time the reader begins a new sentence, the brain is relatively rested and ready for new information. That information is more likely to be understood and trusted.

It is also more likely to be remembered. Not everyone knows that the first sentence of "A Tale of Two Cities" is not as given above. Here is the actual quote:

> It was the best of times, it was the worst of times, it was the age of wisdom, it was the age of foolishness, it was the epoch of belief, it was the epoch of incredulity, it was the season of Light, it was the season of Darkness, it was the spring of hope, it was the winter of despair, we had everything before us, we had nothing before us, we were all going direct to Heaven, we were all going direct the other way—in short, the period was so far like the present period, that some of its noisiest authorities insisted on its being received, for good or for evil, in the superlative degree of comparison only.

If you're being paid by the word, write as Dickens did. (Though Dickens was not, in fact, paid by the word.)

If you want your sentences remembered, keep them short.

Sentences within sentences

One of the miracles of grammar is that it allows you to embed things within other things. Nouns (*France*) can be part of noun phrases (*the capital of France*). Sentences (*Paris is lovely*) can be part of larger sentences (*Pierre thinks that Paris is lovely*). This makes a vast variety of structures possible.

Possible, but not necessarily desirable:

> Opponents of Recep Tayyip Erdogan, Turkey's president, said that his declaration that ten Western ambassadors were "personae non gratae" and would be expelled from the country was an attempt to distract the public from the country's economic woes.

This is not an extremely long sentence, but its structure makes it harder to read than it should be. That's because some of its grammatical pieces are extremely long.

The base structure is *Opponents of Recep Tayyip Erdogan said that X was an attempt to distract the public from the country's economic woes*. Simple enough. The problem is that X stands for *his declaration that ten Western ambassadors were "personae non gratae" and would be expelled from the country*, a lumbering noun phrase with its own complex structure. The reader has to work all this out while reading.

The trick, again, is to break it up. If you want to highlight the president's action first, try:

> Recep Tayyip Erdogan, Turkey's president, declared ten Western ambassadors "personae non gratae" and said they would be expelled from the country. Opponents said he was trying to distract the public from Turkey's economic woes.

If you want to reverse the order, try:

> Opponents of Recep Tayyip Erdogan, Turkey's president, said he was trying to distract the public from the country's economic woes. Their criticism came after he declared ten Western ambassadors "personae non gratae" and said they would be expelled from Turkey.

Either way, break up the Russian-doll nesting of these sentences.

Passive versus active

The default structure of an English sentence is called svo by linguists because in most sentences the Subject, Verb and Object come in that order: *I shot the sheriff, Harry met Sally*. Sentences have a subject (typically the "doer"). Then comes the verb, which is in effect a comment of some kind on the subject (such as what it is, or what it is doing). Finally, some verbs take a direct object (shot *the sheriff*, met *Sally*).

But the subject is not always the agent of the sentence. Look back at the first sentence of the last paragraph. The subject is a noun phrase, *The default structure of an English sentence*. But this isn't "doing" anything. Who is the doer, and what is the action? The agent here is *linguists*, and the action is *call*. This sentence is in the *passive voice*.

In the active voice this would be *Linguists call the default structure of an English sentence svo*. Here the linguists are both subject and the agent. But in a passive sentence, subject and agent are no longer the same. *The shop was destroyed by vandals* has "the shop" as its subject, but not its agent. (A shop, after all, can't do anything.) The vandals are the agent, but not the subject.*

The passive is perfectly grammatical. But there are good reasons why you should prefer the active. It is more direct, shorter and simpler. The active is the default, and so easier to process.

The passive also allows for evasion. In the "short passive" you omit any mention of the agent at all: *The shop was destroyed* or *Funds were embezzled*. Passives allow the illusion of having revealed something without actually naming the perpetrators, much less holding them to account. This is the reason many commentators hold it in disdain. When a journalist writes that *protesters were killed*, the reader understandably wants to know who killed them.

Language mavens also dislike the passive because of its association with certain unloved genres. Academics adore the passive. Read a report of a scientific experiment and you will hunt in vain for *I did the following...* Rather, you will find *the following was done*, almost as though the study performed itself. Other forms of writing, notably that of bureaucrats (*the following three items are required...*), are full of passives too.

Academics want to keep the focus on the work rather than themselves. And bureaucrats may want their rules to appear as though handed down from on high, rather than issued by them. But disembodied, agentless language is off-putting. Readers search for, but never find, clear statements about who did what to whom.

Occasionally, to be sure, the passive is a better choice:

---

* For readers interested in more, a note that is beyond the main discussion: the differences here involve *syntax* versus *semantics*. *Syntax* involves how pieces of a sentence fit together; *semantics* is the study of meaning. *Subject* and *object* are syntactic terms. *Agent* and *patient*, not well known outside academia, are semantic ones. *The shop was destroyed by vandals* and *Vandals destroyed the shop* have the same meaning but different syntax. In the first, *the shop* is the subject but the patient. In the second, *vandals* are the subject and the agent. Subject and agent are aligned in the active voice, but not in the passive.

- **To preserve focus.** If you are writing about Abraham Lincoln it makes sense to say that "He was on the verge of moving on to reunite the country when *he was assassinated in April 1865*." Only if you want to shift focus to the killer should you write "*when John Wilkes Booth assassinated him in April 1865*."
- **To preserve flow.** Readers usually expect information in the order "old, then new". If you have mentioned something in a previous sentence, it often makes sense to make it the subject of the next sentence, even if that requires a passive. "The High Ball entertained regulars at the corner of 5th Avenue and 5th Street for decades. But last month *it was demolished* to make way for condos."
- **When the agent is unknown or unimportant.** In the sentence about Lincoln above, you may assume the reader knows Booth was his assassin, or you may simply not want to talk about him. The passive allows you to skip over him efficiently. In the High Ball example, the reader does not care who did the demolishing.

The passive voice is not the same thing as "vagueness". *Someone made mistakes* is vague—but it is in the active voice. *Mistakes have plagued this administration* is similarly squirrelly—but also active. Not all unclear sentences are grammatical passives. (Some pundits propose calling such pseudo-passives "weasel voice".)

Meanwhile, *Mistakes were made by Stevie in accounting* is perfectly clear about who made the mistakes—but it is passive. So if you refer to the *passive voice* to call out someone trying to wriggle out of culpability, make sure you are talking about a genuine grammatical passive.

Avoiding ambiguity

The horse raced past the barn fell. At first the sentence makes no sense. But if you keep trying, you may be able to see how it does. Two tiny words would save you that effort: "The horse *that was* raced past the barn fell."

As you read a sentence, your brain is constantly trying to identify phrases and clauses. These units give rise to meaning. But many strings of words are ambiguous; they could be understood several different ways. This is the case with *The horse raced past the barn*, which can be a complete sentence, or a noun phrase (meaning "the horse that was raced past the barn").

Memory is too limited to simultaneously consider all possible meanings. Instead, when you encounter "the horse raced past the barn" you do a quick calculation of the most likely meaning. Since horses frequently race, the first three words make you think that "race" is the main verb. Only when the real main verb, "fell", arrives at the end does the reader realise that the first guess must have been wrong, at which point they must re-read. And a sentence that has to be read twice is a failure.

Even apart from trick sentences, ambiguities often arise naturally, too. What does the headline *Swiss Watch Exports Rise* mean? Were the Swiss (people) watching exports rise? (Journalists like to use "watch" in headlines like *Spain Watches Tourist Numbers Fall*.) Or were exports rising in the category of a famous Swiss product, the wristwatch?

Ambiguities like these have two causes. One is grammatical. In the noun phrase "The horse raced past the barn", English allows you to omit words: "The horse [that was] raced past the barn". But in this case, you shouldn't. They provide structural information. Specifically, *that* is useful. As soon as you have read "The horse *that*..." you know that a relative clause (telling you which horse) is coming. Omitting the "that" denies the reader a crucial signal. So as you write, you should trim most words you can. But don't trim more than you can. Those little, unlovely functional words help you avoid ambiguity.

The role of punctuation

Many punctuation rules are quite arbitrary, and have little to do with meaning. *The Economist*, for example, makes certain choices for consistency (see Chapter 7 for details, including on how to order them) without any need to prescribe them to all the world.

But a small few punctuation choices really do have an impact on meaning. Here are the most important marks, and how to think about them.

The **full stop** should be your most frequent recourse. It is humble but powerful. It signals that a sentence is at an end and the reader can clear their mind, file away the information and begin on the next. By breaking up long sentences, full stops also help avoid all sorts of grammatical problems.

The **semicolon** is controversial. Some writers love it; others hate it. Its main job is to connect two independent clauses without need for an *and* or *but*. It signals that the relationship between two clauses is closer than that between separate sentences. As used above, for example, it signifies the balance between two sides of a love-hate opposition. It seems to hover between "and" and "but". This ambiguity can be useful, but should not be overdone. Readers want you to tell them how ideas are connected, not to leave them to guess.

The **colon** is a dramatic device: it says that something is about to happen. It does more than link two ideas. It is the pivot between promising something and delivering it. If this promise-then-delivery function is not fulfilled, you are trying to jazz up your prose unnecessarily. Use a full stop.

The **comma** has so many functions that in any comprehensive guide to punctuation its entry is by far the longest. It was originally a breathing mark, designed to indicate a place for a short pause while reading aloud. That is one reason it is so tricky to use: not all people pause in the same place. (The comma in *Frankly, I don't give a damn* is optional, for example.) The most important hard-and-fast rule with commas is to avoid using them to join two independent sentences (the "comma splice"). Though this sometimes appears in ultra-brief formulations like *Man proposes, God disposes*, unless you are aiming for a similar literary effect, use a semicolon, or a conjunction: *Man proposes, but God disposes*. Finally, *The Economist* does not use the serial comma, the last one in *red, white, and blue*. More on commas in Chapter 7.

The **dash** is like the colon in that it is dramatic—and therefore easily overused. Dashes in pairs can set off an aside—like this—but this attention-grabbing device should be saved for when there is something truly worthy of attention. Otherwise a pair of commas is better. A good rule of thumb is no more than one dash or pair of dashes in a paragraph. And if you find that you have dashes in every paragraph, consider replacing some of them. (Use the long dash, known as the em-dash, which is as long as the letter m is wide.)

Finally, the **hyphen** has various uses, but an important one is showing that several words should be taken together as a unit. When a phrase like *interest rates* stands alone, it needs no hyphen, but when it is used to modify another word, it acts like a single word itself, and therefore gets a hyphen: *interest-rate rises*. This guides the reader in interpreting structure. If you're careful to write *high-school teachers*, there is no chance of *high school teachers* being misinterpreted as *high school-teachers*.

Other common confusions

Whom

Whom is an object pronoun, meaning it can be the direct or indirect object of a verb. In this it is like *him*, *her* or *me*. In deciding between *who* or *whom*, try phrasing your sentence as a declaration. *Who(m) did you see?*, stated as a declaration, becomes *You saw who(m)*. If you would replace *who(m)* with *him*, then you want *whom*.

That said, "whom" appears increasingly fusty in certain contexts (*Whom do you love?*). If it feels odd, best to re-word entirely.

Sentences like *She is the candidate who(m) we think will win* are confusing. Ask yourself what role *who(m)* is playing in the relative clause: *who(m) we think will win*. Here, the correct choice is *who*, because *who* is the subject of the clause. *Who*, like *he* and *she*, is a subject pronoun. You wouldn't say *we think her will win* so don't say *whom will win*.

In these cases, another way to get the solution is to put mental brackets around "we think": *She is the candidate who (we think) will win*.

Between you and I

Prepositions (like *between*) are followed by object pronouns: *me*, *you*, *him*, *her*, *us*, *them*, *whom*. This holds true whether one thing follows the preposition, or several do. *Me* shouldn't become *I* in these cases. If you'd say *to me*, you should say *to you and me*. The same applies to *between you and me*.

Singulars, plurals and subject-verb agreement

Singular subjects get a singular verb, with an -s at the end. Plural subjects get a verb with no -s. This rule is usually easy to follow.

But people can be thrown in cases like *What better evidence that snobbery and elitism still holds back ordinary British people?* The subject here is *snobbery and elitism*. So the verb should be plural: *hold*.

Or take *Examples from the career of the late Elvis Presley shows that...* Once again the subject (*examples*) is plural. But another noun (*Elvis Presley*) is closer to the verb, and so can throw writers off. Don't be fooled by another noun that happens to be nearby.

Words ending in -ics for an academic discipline or the topic in the abstract are singular: *politics, optics, economics, physics*, etc. *Politics is the art of the possible. Economics is his worst subject. Physics attracts a certain kind of mind.* But when preceded by *the*, these are often plural: *The politics of Germany are about to be shaken up. The dynamics of the dynasty are dysfunctional.*

Other -ics that do not represent a field of knowledge or abstract idea are ordinary plurals: *basics, graphics, hysterics, antics, prophylactics, tactics*, etc.

Many nouns make it tricky to know whether to treat them as singular or plural. A football team may act as a unit when it is playing well, and like 11 people who just met (or who hate each other) on a bad day. But British usage is to treat *Liverpool* as a plural when on the field: *Liverpool are winning*. With American teams, though, you may write *Cleveland is winning* (or *The Cleveland Browns are winning*). When another noun (like *the team, the squad*) is used, use the singular (*the team has just won another championship*).

But to describe *Liverpool* as a club or a business, use the singular: *Liverpool has had a bad financial year*. Similarly, a government, a party, a company (whether *Tesco* or *Marks & Spencer*) and a partnership (*Latham & Watkins*) are all *it* and take a singular verb. So does a country, even if its name looks plural. Thus *The Philippines has a congressional system, as does the United States; the Netherlands does not. The United Nations* is singular too.

For a subject not covered here or in Part 2, go by the sense—that is, whether the collective noun stands for a unified entity (*The council was elected in March, The staff is loyal*) or for its constituents: (*The council are confused and divided, The staff are at each other's throats*).

Long subjects with unnecessary commas

Long subjects do not need to be followed by a comma. Some writers put one in sentences like *Tragedies such as the wars that ravaged the countries of the former Yugoslavia in the 1990s, suggest that peacekeepers are best deployed early*, because of a perceived need to pause after such a long opening phrase. But nonetheless, no comma goes here. Everything from "Tragedies" to "1990s" is a single noun phrase. You can replace it with "they". This shows that the comma isn't needed. You wouldn't write *They, suggest that peacekeepers are best deployed early*. (That said, consider rephrasing long sentences so that readers don't have to hold on quite so long for the verb.)

Parallelism

Items in a list should be in the same grammatical form: *I like swimming, hiking and biking*, not *I like swimming, hiking and to bike*. The items can be all gerunds (-ing forms that act as nouns, like *swimming*), infinitives (*to swim, to hike and to bike*) or noun phrases (*the ocean, back-country hikes and the odd death-defying descent on a mountain bike*). But do not mix and match.

This is easy in short sentences, but people often lose sight of parallelism in more complex ones: *We will spend the next quarter researching the market, consolidating product lines, and will update software as well*. This should be *We will spend the next quarter researching the market, consolidating product lines and updating software*. Or you can break up the list and make two clauses: *We will spend the next quarter researching the market and consolidating product lines, and we will update software as well*.

Co-ordinations involving *Both/and* and *either/or* require the items that follow to be parallel in form: *both for the sake of their inhabitants and their neighbours* (*The Economist*, June 2021) is wrong. It should be *for the sake of both their inhabitants and their neighbours*. (Or *both for the sake of their inhabitants and for the sake of their neighbours*, but this is wordier.)

Asides set off by commas

Many people forget the second comma in *Joe Bloggs, an MP and a bird-watching aficionado is the honorary chairman of the Royal Society for the Protection of Birds...* There should be a comma after *aficionado*.

"Fused participles", or possessives followed by gerunds

The present participle—the verb form ending in -ing—is so called because it participates in, or shares the quality of, different parts of speech. In *Snoring is a sign of poor sleep*, the word *snoring* (another gerund) acts like a noun. In *He was snoring when his wife elbowed him in the back of the head*, it is more like a verb.

What to do, then, with *She was awoken by ____ snoring?* Both *his snoring* and *him snoring* are grammatical, despite centuries of dispute by grammarians. Prefer the possessive form, *by his snoring*, where possible. But this rule is not absolute: there is a difference in focus between *They heard him singing* and *They heard his singing*.

Subjunctives

The past subjunctive is used for hypothetical or otherwise unreal statements. It has just one irregular form: Reb Tevye should have sung *If I were a rich man*, not *If I was*. This affects just one verb, *to be*, and only in the *I* and *he/she* forms: *if I were, if she were*. It also follows hypothetical *as if* and *as though*: *He speaks as though he were an expert (but he is not)*.

Not every *if* is followed by the subjunctive. In an open possibility rather than a hypothetical, what follows is *was*: *If he was at the scene, the cameras will have footage of him*. The same goes for the simple past in sentences like *He was asked if he was afraid* (not *if he were afraid*).

The present subjunctive is different. This form involves some kind of entreaty, requirement, hope, prohibition or similar. It exists in frozen expressions like *God **save** the queen, So **be** it, Till death **do** you part, God **shed** his grace on thee*. In modern forms, these would be *May God save the queen, May it be so, Until death does part you* and *May God shed his grace on you*.

The hallmark of a present subjunctive is that in the third-person singular, the verb loses its -s: *God shed his grace on thee* is an entreaty, while *God sheds his grace on thee* is a fact. The verb *to be* is again special. Its subjunctive is *be*: *So be it*.

Outside archaic expressions, the subjunctive is rare in Britain, but is in frequent use in America, where it is called for by certain verbs, including *demand, require, request, recommend, decree*, etc:

> *She demands that each employee arrive at nine o'clock*
> *The law requires that a decree be printed in the official journal*

Do not write these with the indicative (that is, the usual -s form):

> *She demands that each employee arrives at nine o'clock*
> *The law requires that a decree is printed in the official journal*

But the subjunctive is arch-looking in British English. It is best rephrased. You can add *should* to the subjunctive form to make it *She demanded that each employee **should arrive** at nine o'clock*. Or better yet, rephrase it: *She required each employee to arrive at nine o'clock*.

Split infinitives

The idea that nothing may be put between *to* and a verb, as in *to disdainfully split an infinitive*, was first proclaimed in the early 1800s. It was a mistake. The split infinitive had been present in English literature since the 14th century without being labelled incorrect.

But this so-called rule made it into many popular grammars that followed, until it seemed virtually unkillable. H.W. Fowler called the prohibition a "superstition" in his magisterial "Dictionary of Modern English Usage" of 1926. George Bernard Shaw railed against editors who moved his modifiers to avoid the split. Serious grammarians have always known it to be a myth. But it is a myth repeated so often that many readers have internalised a dislike of split infinitives. Some style guides recommend avoiding them on this basis alone, while admitting there is nothing ungrammatical about them.

There are sentences with no good alternative. If you write *researchers demonstrated how wirelessly to hack a car made by Jeep*, as *The Economist* did in 2016, you appear to be answering the question "Just how wirelessly should one hack a car?" We meant *researchers demonstrated how to wirelessly hack a car made by Jeep*. As Geoffrey Pullum, a syntactician at the University of Edinburgh, wrote in response,

The Economist has advocated evidence-based inquiry and intellectual freedom since 1843. Why submit to an adverb-positioning policy founded on dogmatism? The need for clarity should overrule superstitious dread of the split infinitive.

As another reader chided us,

The Economist seems increasingly to prefer actively to write in a way destined consistently to irritate and jar; presumably, so as clearly to demonstrate its commitment consistently to avoid splitting the infinitive.

As this parody shows, avoiding split infinitives by merely moving the adverb one word to the left usually results in confusing manglings. Moving the adverb one word to the right is sometimes a bit better, but often just as bad. The former sentence is hopeless as *Researchers demonstrated how to hack wirelessly a car made by Jeep*.

You can put the adverb at the very end of the sentence if it is short enough. This is often the best solution. But with longer sentences this is not possible: consider *Researchers demonstrated how to hack a car made by Jeep wirelessly*. This gives the impression of a car made wirelessly by the people at Jeep.

Far better is to let good sense reign: put modifiers where they are clearest and strongest. That is sometimes between *to* and its verb. If you are afflicted with an inability to do so, recast the entire sentence, rather than merely moving the adverb by one word and ruining it.

Sentence-ending prepositions

This rule is not observed by quite as many as the split-infinitive myth, but many people nonetheless believe that you cannot end a sentence with a preposition. They are wrong. The prohibition began life as a musing on why it was better style not to do so, in a seventeenth-century essay by John Dryden. The poet's pronouncement found its way into influential grammar books, first as a preference and then as a "rule", until it became another of the many things that "everyone knows". But *It's not the things that people don't know; it's the things they don't know that ain't so.*

You can say *the things about which they were speaking*, or *the things they were speaking about.* Both are acceptable, but the latter is more natural, and usually the better choice. Churchill did not actually describe twisted sentences avoiding terminal prepositions as *arrant nonsense up with which I will not put*. But he should have.

Conjunctions at the beginning of sentences

This is another schoolroom shibboleth. As the last sentence of the previous section shows, there is nothing wrong with starting a sentence with *and*, *or*, or *but*. The prohibition against doing so may have begun with teachers trying to correct students out of beginning each new sentence with *And*... And while this is sound advice—you shouldn't start every sentence with a conjunction—there is no reason to avoid ever doing so. These little words (as their name suggests) link things together, and are common in a natural style.

Dangling modifiers

Honestly, he's a liar. Frankly, she's being disingenuous. Seriously, he's a clown. Unfortunately, he won the lottery. Hopefully, they'll give up in despair. A strong prohibition against "dangling modifiers"—bits of expository language that do not modify the subject of the sentence, but which can be misinterpreted as doing so—would make all of these sentences incoherent.

Many dangling modifiers go unnoticed: they have been documented throughout literature, great nonfiction writing, the Declaration of Independence (and *The Economist*). They are especially common in speech: *Speaking as an old friend, there has been a disturbing tendency in statements emanating from Peking to question the good faith of President Reagan* (Richard Nixon).

The problem is that in some cases, dangling modifiers invite absurd readings. This is particularly so when the modifiers are participles, verb forms ending in -ing or (usually) -ed. *Walking down the street, it started to rain* ("it", whatever it is, was not walking down the street). *Born in poverty, his success surprised even him.* (His success was not born in poverty.) Readers naturally want these participles to apply to the first noun they find. When the noun is the wrong one, they stop in confusion (and sometimes dash off a letter to the editor). Reword to forestall these misreadings.

The prohibition on dangling modifiers is sometimes extended to non-participles. Adverbs like *Unfortunately* and other grammatical devices are thought to have to modify the verb of the main clause. They do not necessarily.

But again, be vigilant. You may (even unintentionally) achieve humorous effect, like the wag who described the excitement awaiting two new giant pandas at the Edinburgh zoo: *Though overweight, uninterested in sex, and notorious for their very poor diet, they were still very glad to see the pandas arrive.*

In other cases, a dangler could be shockingly libellous, as in a draft sentence that fortunately never appeared in *The Economist*: *Having carried out two executions within a month and with another man scheduled to die on April 29th, Amnesty International said there were "deep flaws" in Singapore's use of the death penalty.* Fortunately, this was rescued by an editor at the last moment. Amnesty is, in fact, stringently opposed to stringing people up.

Singular "they"

English lacks a pronoun that refers to a subject that is anonymous, generic, unknown or unimportant: *Everyone has ___ own opinion, Someone left ___ umbrella here, Everyone should bring ___ spouse, unless ___ ___ unavailable.*

An old-fashioned solution is that *he/him/his* is English's generic, sexless pronoun: *Everyone has his own opinion.* But this has too many strikes against it. *He* is not truly neutral. First, when you hear *Everyone has his own opinion*, psychologists have shown, you picture a man, not a woman. Even those who still insist *he* is generic would probably balk at sentences like *whoever wins the contest between Rishi Sunak and Liz Truss will have his hands full.*

The simplest fix is to make the referent plural. This makes the problem disappear, since plural *they* is genderless. So instead of *A writer should always sleep on his draft before sending it off*, try *Writers should always sleep on their drafts before sending them off.*

Another trick is to eliminate any gendered pronouns you can: *A writer should always sleep on a draft before sending it off.* This is the most elegant solution when you want to invoke the image of a single writer.

A once-popular fix was to use *he or she, his or her* and so on. It can still work in isolation, as in *whoever takes over will have his or her hands full.*

He or she, though, grates upon repetition: *He or she which hath no stomach to this fight, let him or her depart; his or her passport shall be made, and crowns for convoy put into his or her purse. We would not die in that man's or woman's company that fears his or her fellowship to die with us.*

A far better alternative is available. Singular *they* is sometimes derided as the successor to *he or she*, modern political correctness run amok. It is not, unless the 14th century is "modern" and Shakespeare, the King James Bible and the Oxford English Dictionary are sources of political correctness. Singular *they* has been in continuous use in English since at least 1375, according to the OED, and so is even older than supposedly sex-neutral *he.*

Singular *they* (and *them* and *their*) is particularly natural in reference to an antecedent like *someone, anyone, no one, everyone. Someone left their purse here. Anyone can rise to the top here if they work hard enough. No one likes having their opinions questioned. Everyone has their own idea of how this began.* These are acceptable. In *The Economist's* obituary of Roger Ailes in 2017, we wrote *If somebody got in his face, he'd get in their face.* This can be written no other way.

Singular *they* can also be used to refer back to *a student, each professor, the careful reader* and so on: *A young lawyer hoping to become a partner must be prepared to sacrifice their personal life.* But these are usually better pluralised, since *a young lawyer* calls to mind a specific person, with whom the *they* can clash more than it does with an impersonal *someone.* Hence: *Young lawyers hoping to become a partner must be prepared to sacrifice their personal lives.*

The "false possessive"

There are many readers and editors convinced that a rule against the "false possessive" prohibits phrases like *London's National Theatre*, since the theatre does not belong to London ("National" is right there in the name).

This is not a true grammatical error. The *'s*, known as the *possessive* but really the *genitive* inherited from Anglo-Saxon, implies many kinds of relationships beyond ownership: possession (*Joan's car*), part-to-whole (*Geoff's arm*), relationship (*Eva's father*), source (*Henry's drumming*), creation (*Jack's films*), action (*Willie's singing*), attribute (*Roger's age*) and so on. This can also be expressed with an *of* phrase in many cases, but in other cases cannot.

That said, if you mean a mere location, prefer *Piccadilly Circus in London* over *London's Piccadilly Circus*. Further, *'s* is often cacophonous (*Congress's*) or awkward (as in *international banking number-crunchers' best estimates are*). These are best replaced with an *of* phrasing (the wishes *of Congress*, the best estimates *of international banking number-crunchers*).

"Which" v "that"

A relative clause is one that gives more information about a noun recently mentioned. Some relative clauses give critical information, specifying which noun is meant: *The car that he bought from the proceeds of his fraud was impounded*. In this case, he might have more than one car, and the relative clause tells you which was impounded. This is a "restrictive" relative clause.

But in *The car, which he bought from the proceeds of his fraud, was impounded*, the relative clause is an additional bit of information. It is not picking one car from a set. This is a "non-restrictive relative".

A century ago, H.W. Fowler mused that it might be simpler if only *that* was used in the first type, and only *which* with the second. This was not a rule but a suggestion. But the rule caught on in America, where it made its way into William Strunk's and E.B. White's "Elements of Style", and thence into many teachers' and editors' minds.

This is nonetheless another "rule" that does not deserve the name. Non-restrictive clauses should not begin in *that* (*The car, that he bought with the proceeds of his fraud, was impounded*, is jarring.) But restrictive clauses may indeed begin with *which* (*The car which he bought from the proceeds of his fraud was impounded*).

Commas (in writing) and rhythm (in speech) do the work of making clear what kind of relative clause is meant. Franklin Roosevelt was saying nothing incorrect when he called December 7th 1941 *a date which will live in infamy*. And the King James Bible was not committing a grammatical sin in referring to *our father which art in Heaven*. This specifies which father is meant: the man upstairs, not Dad back at home.

May, might

The verbs *can*, *will* and *may* have the past-tense forms *could*, *would* and *might*.

> *He **says** he **can** go* v *He **said** he **could** go*
> *She **says** she **will** stay* v *She **said** she **would** stay*
> *They **say** it **may** be a problem* v *They **said** it **might** be a problem*

Of the three, only *may* and *might* are typically confused. In the past tense, use *might*. Do not write *He said they may even win*, but *He said they might even win*.

Confusion also arises because *could*, *would* and *might* also have present-tense uses. These are more remote from reality than *can*, *will* and *may*. *She can play the tuba* is a fact, but *She could play the tuba* only hints at the possibility (if she practised harder, if only there were one available).

So use *may* when some confidence is intended: *She may play the tuba (if the mood strikes)*. And use *might* when you are less certain: *She might play the tuba (but I doubt it)*.

By the same token, use *may* for an open possibility: *I may have called him a liar (but I'd had a few, and I'm not certain)*. Use *might* for counterfactuals: *I might have called him a liar (but we had both had a few, and I was not feeling lucky)*.

"By that test," wrote *The Economist* (March 19th 2011), "the West let down the Bahrainis: sterner talk from Mr Obama may have deterred their attackers." As it stands, that suggests Mr Obama provided sterner talk and it possibly deterred the attackers. In fact, the opposite had happened. The sterner talk that might have deterred the attackers had been absent. The *may* should have been the counterfactual *might*.

Do not write *He might call himself an ardent free-market banker, but he did not reject a government rescue*. Since he does call himself a free marketeer, this should be *He may call himself an ardent free-market banker, but he did not reject a government rescue*.

Inanimate "whose"

Who has the possessive form *whose*, but *what* has no uncontroversial possessive.

Nonetheless, you should not fear sentences like the observation from Victor Hugo in its most famous translation: "Nothing else in the world...not all the armies...is so powerful as *an idea whose time has come*." The alternative, *an idea the time of which has come*, is unbearably wooden.

In any case, *an idea whose time has come* is perfectly grammatical. *Whose* is the original genitive of *what* and later of *which*, as well as of *who*. The use of *whose* with an inanimate noun has been in steady use since at least the 14th century, and appears in the Bible, Shakespeare, Milton, Conrad and endless other historical sources. Knowledgeable commentators from H.W. Fowler through Eric Partridge to Bryan Garner have no qualms about it.

Rephrase with *of which* where you can, but not when this produces something clumsy.

Rulings on individual words (eg, singular or plural *data*) can be found in Chapter 6. But don't be overwhelmed by their number. Two pieces of guidance are worth repeating here. Use the full stop everywhere you can. And write as though speaking to a friend rather than aiming to impress. You already know most of the grammar you need. Doing these two things will keep most grammar troubles from ever arising.

4

The bottom line: writing with numbers

"The numbers don't lie," goes a cliché. But another cliché distinguishes three kinds of falsehood: "lies, damned lies and statistics". Numbers certainly can mislead, whether intentionally or unintentionally.

This guide cannot introduce all the complexity of numerical reasoning, including in the specialist areas of business, finance, economics and science. But writers often fall into the same set of traps. Here is a brief guide around them.

Numbers are powerful—a single statistic can justify an article in *The Economist*. But it must be well deployed. Do not bamboozle the reader with a stream of numbers; as with your words, choose them carefully. As a rule of thumb avoid having more than two numbers per paragraph. And be especially careful not to deaden your intros with them.

General numeracy

Correlation and causation

First and foremost, *correlation is not causation*. If you see umbrellas on the bus in the morning, and it rains later that day, the umbrellas did not cause the rain. Two figures may well be related (as they are here) but the causation may well run the other way, a third factor may cause both phenomena, or coincidence may be at play.

No academic publication worth its peer review will fail to take this into account. So if you refer to a study that shows levels of depression increasing at the same time as increased use of smartphones, dig carefully. Read the original study, not just the press release (much less someone else's write-up). See how carefully the researchers controlled for other factors that might also have caused rising depression: economic conditions, other things that smartphone users might do (such as play video games or forgo in-person contact), etc.

Pressure groups, in particular, will often try to influence you by implying that correlation is causation. When quoting a study published by such a group, which will usually not go through the (often quite adversarial) review process that academic work does, you should be doubly sceptical, and present any such findings with suitable caveats.

Statistical significance

Causation is not the same thing as *statistical significance*. The latter refers to researchers' estimation of the probability that the two variables they are looking at are not correlated by mere chance. The usual test in the social sciences is to show that the likelihood of a coincidence is less than 5%. This seems like an impressive finding: that the researchers' conclusion is 95% likely to be correct. Many people read that as "near certainty".

The more data that researchers have, the more they can rule out chance. If you flip a coin ten times and get heads six, you have too little data to suggest the coin is weighted unfairly. If you flip it 1,000 times and it comes up heads 600, you can be almost certain it is. Beware of concluding too much from studies based on few data points.

Even in well-designed studies, one in 20 papers near the 5% threshold—thousands published every year—are the product of chance. A way to correct for the flaws of individual studies is to rely on a *meta-study*, an analysis of many different individual pieces of research, using statistical methods to combine their results and make more solid conclusions than any single one could.

And it is important to remember the many reasons that a finding purporting to be statistically significant may still warrant scepticism. Because of the 5% gold standard, suspiciously many papers are published whose value for p, the standard figure for statistical significance, is right around .05. This means that many papers with good results just above .05 may not be published, and more disturbingly, that many researchers may be re-running and subconsciously massaging their study design until *p* reaches the magical threshold, a practice sometimes called "p-hacking".

A finding of statistical significance means that one variable is almost certainly having an effect on another. But it says nothing about how big that effect is—"significant" here does not mean "large". So look out for *effect size*. Parents' height is correlated with that of their children, but not perfectly. Other factors, including nutrition and random variation, play a role too. When describing such correlations, try to give an idea of how strongly they hold.

Sometimes a figure is given of *explained variance*: a scientific study might say *around 35% of the variance in children's height is explained by the variance in their parents' height*. Some statisticians quibble with this language, which has a technical meaning that can mislead laypeople. The important thing is not to confuse significance (how likely it is a connection exists) with effect size (how strongly one variable affects the other).

Bear *baselines* in mind when writing about changes. If eating lamb chops doubles your risk of a certain cancer you might swear off the things for life, unless you subsequently read that the original risk of that cancer is extremely low. Doubling that risk leaves the chance extremely low.

Averages: mean, median and mode

Be careful with the word *average*. It is usually best to specify whether you mean *mean*, *median* or (least often) *mode*.

- The *mean* is found by adding up all the figures in a series and dividing by the number of figures.
- The *median* is found by lining up the values from highest to lowest and choosing the one in the middle (or averaging the two in the middle, if an even number).
- The *mode* is the number that appears most frequently.

The *mean* is what most readers associate with an average, as it is good for a wide range of applications. But the "average" human being has a mean of approximately one breast and one testicle, an absurdist illustration of the way means can mislead. Here is where the *mode* gives a very different impression: the modal number of testicles is zero (because there are more women than men).

The *median* can be associated with the idea of a "typical" value. Imagine a street with 20 houses ranging from $300,000 to $400,000 in value. It is easy to imagine the typical value on the street: the mean and median are likely to be similar. Now imagine a mansion at the end of the block, worth $10m. This would drag the mean sharply upwards, but the median little. In this case, the mean would be badly misleading, describing a house of about $800,000 that nobody lives in. The median here is a better choice when describing the "average" house.

So when you choose your average, choose carefully. And when you report others' averages, make sure you know whether they chose an illuminating or a deceptive measure.

Context and comparability

A bit of care with your numerical language will make life easier for your reader. Use round fractions, rather than percentages, where you can (say something fell by half, or doubled, rather than fell by 50% or rose by 100%). It is much easier to read that "a third of Britain's housing stock is more than 20 years old" than that "36% of Britain's housing stock is more than 20 years old".

Journalists are fond of big numbers: *Russia generates $1bn a day from energy exports. $100bn in illicit money is laundered in Britain each year. Americans spend $3.6trn a year on health care.* But readers start losing the ability to make any sense of numbers with six zeros or more. Push into billions and trillions and they certainly need help from context. A number may look impressive, and then turn out to be less so when contextualised.

It helps little to give some overused adjective like *eye-watering*, *eye-popping* or *whopping* to describe such figures. Instead, consider: What proportion of a country's economy does the health care account for? How has it grown in recent years? How does it compare with other countries? This can all be put succinctly: *Health care consumes 18% of GDP in America, equivalent to $3.6trn a year. In other rich countries the share is around 10%, but rising as populations age.* Another useful measure is to describe such figures *per person* or similar: *Schools in England spend on average £6,700 per pupil.*

Comparisons can be useful, as in the international kind, *America spends more on defence than the next nine countries combined,* or the domestic one, *Defence accounts for nearly half of all discretionary spending.*

But beware the spurious comparison beloved of journalists, especially of figures that are not commensurate: *At $3trn, Apple's market capitalisation is greater than the GDP of India* is particularly confusing. In economic terms, it compares a stock (the snapshot value of the entire Apple corporation at a moment in time) with a flow (the value of goods and services produced by the Indian economy over a year).

When GDP is compared to a flow at Apple, like revenue (around $380bn in 2021), the comparator is now *Finland*—but turnover isn't an accurate comparator either. Better would be Apple's profits ($30bn). Now the journalist is left making a more sensible but less impressive comparison with *Honduras*. Some economists would add in Apple's wage payments to make the comparison more accurate still, but by now the journalist is left doing too much explaining. Less literary, but more appropriate, is to simply compare like with like.

That is unless you are aiming to be light-hearted. *The Economist's* data team got across the immense success of the song "Gangnam Style" by expressing the time spent watching the YouTube video as multiples of the time taken for other great achievements of humanity. At the time of publication, six times as many hours had been spent on the South Korean mega-hit as were spent on building the world's tallest building, the Burj Khalifa, for example.

Assorted traps

Be consistent in the number of significant figures you give—that is, the number of digits not counting leading zeros. For example, 156,000 rounded to two significant figures is 160,000; 0.00233 is 0.0023. Often, giving two significant figures is enough. If you want a number to make an impact you don't want readers to have to wrangle strings of digits, lest they forget the scale of what you're talking about.

It is easy to slip and think that a 400% increase in some amount means multiplying it by four. Remember that when something *increases by 100%* it *doubles*, and when *by 200%*, it *triples*, and so on. (And avoid *-fold* or be explicit what you mean: some people reckon a *two-fold increase* is a doubling, while others see it as a tripling. Better to say something has doubled or tripled.)

Be careful to distinguish between *percentage* changes and *percentage-point* changes. As a rule, percentage changes have some relationship to an underlying value; percentage-point changes refer to another percentage. If the population of Britain goes from 60m to 65m, it has increased by about 8%. If China's annual growth rate goes from 7% to 5%, then it has fallen by two percentage points (not by 2%).

If America's growth rate goes from 1% to 2%, it is technically correct to say *America's growth rate has increased by 100%* or *has doubled*, but both look strange, especially when the original number is so small. Instead say *America's growth rate has increased by one percentage point.*

Refer to numerical changes in the expected order: old, then new. *America's GDP growth fell from 3.0% in 2018 to 2.2% in 2019.* Writing it the other way round—*America's growth rate fell to 2.2% in 2019, from 3.0% in 2018*—forces the reader to mentally reverse the order of events.

Do not omit significant zeros. *8%* is not the same as *8.0%* in a world of messy figures rounded for publication. 8% could refer to anything from 7.51% to 8.49%. 8.0% refers to figures between 7.95% and 8.049%.

Speed, height, weight and so on are measured in numbers. Slowness, shortness and lightness are not, mathematically speaking. So say *one-third as heavy* rather than *three times lighter*, *half as tall* rather than *twice as short*, etc.

Watch out with *square metres* versus *metres square*. A square room of *ten square metres* is about 3.16 metres on each side. One *ten metres square* is usually understood to mean one with sides of ten metres (and an area of 100 square metres). Since the latter is ambiguous, it is best avoided. Use *square metres* (or specify *ten metres on each side*).

The language of business

Business, finance and economics present particular difficulties for writers. Like all technical subjects, they have their jargon but, with an even bigger stock of half-dead metaphors. Words like *bail-out*, *bubble*, *distressed*, *gap*, *hedge*, *imbalance*, *leverage*, *spread*, *start-up*, *stimulus* and *yield* seem to appear in every sentence of an economist's prose.

The scope for clashes is huge. Throw in some clichés and you soon have *benchmarks*, *flatlining* growth, things *going north*, *green shoots*, *kick-starts*, *level playing-fields*, *spiking prices* and *toxic assets* joining the mix.

Add in such euphemisms as *compensation* (for *pay*), *impairments* (*losses*), *letting people go* (*giving them the boot*), *stretched structures* (*devices deeply in debt*), *sub-investment-grade debt* (*junk bonds*), and the concoction becomes heady.

Next come the misnomers (*sustainable business*, which may well be *going bust*), the neologisms (*mezzanine capital*, *vanilla products*) and the designed-to-be-unintelligible (*collateralised debt obligations*, which are, of course, *structured asset-backed securities*), and the reader is in a state of neo-classical disequilibrium that borders on terminal vital-sign insolvency.

Your goal is to be both accurate and readable. These can sometimes be in tension. For example, Roman Weil of the University of Chicago counsels people never to use the phrase *making money*. He has tallied at least six different things (not including counterfeiting) that the phrase is commonly used to mean, including taking in lots of revenue, making large net profits, seeing assets grow in value, realising the growth in assets by selling them, etc. To an accountant— or a careful reader of financial statements—these are very different things.

Profits, cash and the balance sheet

Revenues are a company's "top line"—how much money has come in from core operations over a quarter or year. It is often loosely referred to as *sales*, but if accuracy matters, *revenue* includes all *sales* as well as some other income. Do not be too impressed if a company crows that revenues are growing briskly. It may be spending a lot of money to make money, so that its losses are growing even faster.

Profits are reported on companies' income statements. (Prefer *profits* to *earnings* unless discussing *earnings per share*, a measure of the attractiveness of a company's stock.) Be clear about which ones you mean. *Gross profits* are revenues minus the cost of the goods sold (including direct labour costs like factory workers).

Operating profits are a more useful measure for many companies, as they take into account wider costs of doing business, including rents, shipping, depreciation of assets and assorted overheads. This figure gives a good idea of whether a business is sustainably profitable. EBITDA, a similar figure much beloved of financial analysts, stands for *earnings* (that is, profits) *before interest, taxes, depreciation and amortisation*. It is an ungainly acronym best replaced with the phrase *gross operating profits*. Watch out on financial statements for *adjusted* EBITDA, which often means the company has produced a customised figure to flatter its results.

Net income is the "bottom line" (literally, the last one on the income statement). It is the fullest account of how much a company has made in a year. But it includes one-off items like payouts from lawsuits, sales of assets and so on. If a company has done something like sell a division in a year, it should not be taken as an indicator of its sustainable ability to make a profit. Net income is the figure used when calculating earnings per share.

Cashflows are not the same things as sales. A company is allowed by accounting rules to book income as earned for a piece of work completed (which counts towards its profits that year). But it may not have the money from the customer yet. (It may, conversely, be paid in advance for work not yet completed, in which case it incurs an accounting liability until the work is done.) Cashflow thus tracks the money actually in and out of the company. *Free cashflow* is a much-watched indicator of how much cash a company has available to pay creditors and investors (after capital investments have been subtracted).

The other important financial statement companies put out is a *balance-sheet*. Unlike the income statement, which measures a period of time like a quarter or a year, the balance-sheet is a snapshot. It lists *assets* (physical and intangible) and *liabilities*, and the difference between the two is by definition *stockholders' equity*. This is the same as *book value*: in effect what would be left for the owners if the company's assets were sold and creditors paid. It is not the same as (and is usually less than) *market capitalisation*, which is the price of the company's shares multiplied by the number of shares. Finally, *enterprise value* comes up in mergers and acquisitions, and adjusts market capitalisation for net debt.

Banks are counterintuitive in accounting terms. When they make a loan they book an asset, because they now have a right to future payments from the borrower. A bank is in trouble when it holds lots of *non-performing loans* (which do not sing or dance and are more crisply referred to as *bad loans*). These are in danger of being *written down* in value or being *written off* entirely. Deposits, on the other hand, are a liability, because they are owed back to the account holder.

And ledger-keeping's language of *debits* and *credits* is counterintuitive to laypeople too. (When accountants add to a cash account, that account is debited, not credited, for example.) So debits and credits are best avoided.

Finance and markets

When in doubt, spell financial terms out in words that laypeople use, or non-experts will not be able to understand your copy. Central banks, therefore, raise rates by a *quarter of a percentage point*, not 25 *basis points*. *Unicorns* are privately held companies worth more than a billion dollars. Tell readers what companies and entities do, eg, that *Goldman Sachs* is *a bank*, even if this is obvious to you. (If *Goldman Sachs, a bank* feels clumsy, give its name on first mention, and refer to it as *the bank* as soon as possible afterwards.) It can be hard to describe sprawling companies, but do your best: *Unilever is a consumer-goods giant*, or *Unilever is a soup-to-soap conglomerate*.

By the same token, try to explain things that are widely known to financial insiders but may confuse outsiders. Just a few words will remind readers why *bond prices rise when interest rates fall* (because already issued bonds at higher rates become more attractive), or that *bond yields* fall when bond prices rise (because yields are calculated by dividing by the price).

A bank's *stockholder's equity* is usually referred to as its *capital*. This can be confusing. It is often written that banks "hold capital", which the layman will interpret as a reference to the bank's *cash reserves*. The two are separate: capital tells you nothing about the breakdown of a bank's assets. To avoid confusion, say a bank is *funding itself with more capital*. This is clunkier but more accurate.

Be careful with the term *reserves*. A bank's reserves usually means its *cash*, including both banknotes in the vault and digital money held with the central bank. But the technical term for the latter is *central-bank reserves*, and sometimes documents will contrast these with physical banknotes, calling only the latter *cash*.

Complicating matters further, a central bank's *foreign-exchange reserves* refers to its foreign-currency assets, digital or physical, which can include things like government bonds denominated in reserve currencies (mostly dollars).

The dismal science

Gross domestic product or GDP is the best yardstick for the size or *output* of an economy. It measures the total value of goods and services that an economy produces. It is to be preferred to other similar measures (*gross value added, gross national income, gross national product*), unless there is a good reason to do otherwise.

One way of measuring GDP is to add up total spending on consumption, investment, government and exports, then subtract imports, which are produced overseas. The result is the market value of GDP at current prices. Things are more complicated when tracking *GDP growth*. That is because growth in total spending, or *nominal GDP*, will reflect inflation as well as increased production. Adjusting for inflation will produce growth in *real GDP*. When writing about economic growth, always use real GDP. If for some reason you use nominal GDP, say so. Most statistics agencies and other publications also follow this rule.

Do not take the equation for calculating GDP as an all-purpose guide for boosting growth. More spending will always boost nominal GDP, all else equal. But the extent to which it boosts real GDP, rather than bringing about more inflation, depends on whether there is *slack* in the economy, such as unemployed workers and underused physical capital. Without slack, extra spending is more likely to boost inflation than output.

Long-run growth is not determined by the spending equation. A government that spent without limit would not find that it made its people rich, and a country that exported but never imported would in effect be giving things away for nothing. Over long stretches, economic growth is driven by *supply-side* factors such as growth in productivity and the labour force.

Be wary of politicians or companies boasting of having boosted the economy by *creating jobs*. If the economy has slack, more hiring probably will boost total employment. But if the economy is tight, it is more likely to shuffle workers and capital around. Whether that is good or bad for GDP depends on whether the new arrangement is more productive.

GDP numbers are usually reported as *seasonally adjusted* ones, to account for, for example, increased economic activity around the Christmas holidays. Be careful not to compare one country's seasonally adjusted figures with another country's unadjusted ones. Since seasonal adjustment is also a default, you need not mention it (but you may need to do so when figures are not seasonally adjusted).

Also be careful with *year-on-year* versus *quarter-on-quarter* or *month-on-month figures*. If GDP rises in the second quarter by 2% year on year, that means it is 2% higher than the second quarter of the previous year. If it rises 2% quarter on quarter, though, it has risen 2% on the previous (ie, the first) quarter of the same year. Such a pace, if sustained for four quarters, would lead to annual growth of over 8%. Some countries, such as Japan and America, report quarterly GDP growth in annualised terms.

It is helpful to compare large numbers to GDP to give readers a sense of scale. But be careful about implying that something is included in GDP. *Remittances*, monies sent from overseas, might be worth 10% of GDP, but will never make up 10% of GDP, because they are not part of the definition, as they are not domestically produced goods or services.

Be careful when averaging growth rates, whether of GDP or anything else. When calculating growth over time (for example, "the production of coffee has grown by an average 3.4% a year since 2013") it is tempting to take the mean of the growth rates for each year. This is incorrect. If something grows by 50% for two years running it will be larger than if it grows by 10% one year and 90% the next, even though the mean of the growth rates is 50% in both cases.

Unemployment is not just the mirror image of *employment.* Unemployment statistics measure the people actively seeking a job but unable to find one. Employment measures the proportion of a population in work. It may be affected not only by formal unemployment, but by people leaving the hunt for a job, women's lower workforce participation or a country's early retirement age.

A country's *trade balance* is the value of its exports minus the value of its imports. This is distinct from its *current-account balance*, which also includes income earned on assets overseas, less domestic income flowing to foreign owners. A *current-account deficit* means a country is a net borrower from abroad; a *current-account surplus* means it is a net lender. Both figures are best expressed as a percentage of GDP. Rich countries are generally better able to cope with large current-account deficits, since they tend to benefit from flows of long-term funding, such as foreign direct investment by companies. Poor countries usually rely more on short-term funding from international investors, which can dry up quickly in a crisis.

The (budget) *deficit* is the difference between what the government takes in (mostly tax revenues) and what it spends (expenditure). Public *debt* is the outstanding stock of money that a government owes. Always specify the type of debt you are talking about: is it household, corporate, public or total debt? And think about whether a given debt level matters. An 80% public debt-to-GDP ratio is worrying for a poor country, less so for a rich one. Governments and firms that have borrowed heavily in foreign currency are at the mercy of movements in their own currency; those such as America that borrow in their own currency do not bear this risk. You also need to consider how soon the debt needs to be paid back (debt *maturity*).

Finally, in keeping with the counterintuitive theme, *public goods* are not things that are good for the public. They are goods and services that cannot be fenced off and that remain just as accessible no matter how many people use them (economists say they are "non-excludable" and "non-rivalrous"). Examples of pure public goods include national defence and official statistics.

The less dismal sciences

Journalists are fond of dressing up their prose with scientific and mathematical terms, which makes writing sound more profound than it is: *optics, calculus, orthogonal, tangential, parsing,* etc. Avoid this temptation, and use the words you would use in ordinary conversation, like *appearances* for *optics* or *calculations* for *calculus* (as in *political calculus*). And if you do use them when writing about science, use them with caution: readers know them too.

Be careful with *exponential growth.* It is not the same as fast growth, and indeed can be quite slow, depending on the exponent in question and where something is in the growth process. Exponential growth describes what bacteria do, for example, when there is nothing to stop their growth. One becomes 2, which become 4, 8, 16, 32 and so on. A number increasing by a steady, even if very large, amount (1,000, 2,000, 3,000, 4,000 on successive days) is going through *linear growth.*

In reporting on health, do not mention a *lower risk of mortality* without qualifiers. The risk of death for living things is exactly 100%. Describe the time period or other frame of reference for the study you are writing about.

A warming world

Global warming refers to rising average global temperatures. *Climate change* refers to broader changes including warming, changing weather, melting ice caps and glaciers, and ocean acidification. *Global heating* is a term adopted by some news organisations to convey a sense of urgency. The urgency is real, but *The Economist* does not use the term.

The anthropogenic causes of climate change can be taken as fact and do not need to be stated in every story about climate change.

Greenhouse-gas emissions are quantified in different ways, leading to some confusion over units. One *tonne of carbon dioxide* (avoid CO_2) is not the same as a *tonne of carbon*. To convert a tonne of carbon to a tonne of carbon dioxide, multiply by 3.67.

A tonne of *carbon-dioxide equivalent* (CO_2e) is something else again. This measures all greenhouse gases but corrects for their warming power (which can be greater or lesser than carbon dioxide) and their staying power in the atmosphere (ditto). Molecule-for-molecule, *methane* warms the planet more than carbon dioxide does, but it has a much shorter lifespan. Any sentence comparing the two needs to specify the time period.

The UN document signed in Paris in 2015 is the *Paris agreement* not the Paris accord. (The UN climate agreement made in Kyoto in 1997 was the *Kyoto protocol*.)

The Paris agreement has temperature targets not emissions targets. Parties to the agreement pledge to "[hold] the increase in the global average temperature to well below 2°C above pre-industrial levels and [pursue] efforts to limit the temperature increase to 1.5°C above pre-industrial levels". *Pre-industrial*, in this context, is understood to mean 1850-1900. Use *Celsius* temperatures, not Fahrenheit, unless quoting someone who does otherwise (and if you do that, give a conversion).

Geoengineering (no hyphen) describes a suite of mechanisms to reduce global temperatures independent of efforts to reduce emissions, such as mechanisms for reflecting the sun's energy back into space before it can warm the planet.

Efforts to reduce greenhouse-gas emissions are known as *mitigation*. Net-zero targets are one example. Projects to help society adapt to the impacts of climate change come under the umbrella of *adaptation*. Sea walls and drought-resistant crops are forms of adaptation.

Ocean acidification is a result of the fact that oceans absorb carbon dioxide. It is not a result of warming. Ocean water is slightly alkaline. Acidification makes it less so, but not *acidic*.

Many writers might find writing about numerical and scientific topics intimidating; after all, it seems easier to be proved wrong if you make a mistake. But if you use numbers that are both accurate and illuminating, your copy is more likely to be taken as well-grounded.

Public companies provide a wealth of figures that they are required by regulators not to manipulate egregiously. Outside analysts (eg, those at banks) can help you make sense of them. National statistics in most countries are put out by serious professionals, and that goes too for the work of the International Monetary Fund, World Bank, OECD and the like. In the sciences, most scholars are happy to talk about their work (and often happy to evaluate that of others, in case you are not sure about the solidity of a study). So even if you feel at sea with figures, you are not alone with them. Pick up the phone or send off an e-mail for help.

5

Then you begin to make it better: editing

Editing—whether done by an editor or writers themselves—should help produce the best version of the document the author set out to write.

That means that if you're the editor, the aim is not to turn it into what you would have written. This is a fine balance. On the one hand, as an editor you are a stand-in for the audience: if you find something confusing, boring or unconvincing, some readers probably will, too. On the other, this is someone else's work, not yours, even if you think you would have done it better. You should aim to rise above personal preference.

When commissioning a piece, explicit guidance about what you would like to see in it, especially with a writer you have not worked with much before, can save both you and the writer disappointment later on. It is far easier to adjust a starting approach than a completed draft.

When the draft arrives, be specific and constructive in your comments. Don't say "I didn't like this part"; say what didn't work. And the use of "you" can feel accusatory, especially when repeated. Editing should not be personal. Note which paragraphs or points don't work, and why.

Ideally, you will work out how to fix any problems you spot. Then, depending on what has been agreed, you can either go ahead and make the change, or give the author a detailed explanation and ask them to do it. If you can see that something is wrong, but not how to fix it, talk it through with the author. You will often find that simply asking what they were trying to say reveals the mismatch between the aim and the result to both of you.

Asking your writer to make changes, rather than making them

yourself, has another benefit: if you hope to work with the writer again, you will be showing them how to give you what you want next time. It may take longer to explain than to make the changes yourself, but this investment of time will pay off later.

Send queries in one go, if possible, rather than peppering the author repeatedly. Consider whether tracked changes or comments (or in-text insertions in ALL CAPS, if they are simple and infrequent enough) will be best. A document with tracked changes from many editors quickly becomes unmanageable.

Don't forget to say what you liked. Generic praise, such as "nice job" or "interesting", is of limited help. Take the time to work out precisely what worked, and say so. Well-chosen words of praise are highly motivating: if you tell a writer that their explanations are beautifully clear, or their introduction snappy or conclusion enlightening, that writer will do more of what you liked next time. Constructive, justified words of praise also make it likely that your criticisms will be taken in the right spirit. Writers will take criticism better if they know you admire their strengths and aren't being spiteful or picky.

Murdering darlings

When you write you should edit yourself as vigorously as possible. You must forget how much work it has taken to get your first draft down. Look dispassionately at what is on the page and do whatever is necessary to make it as good as it can be, even if that means cutting words, sentences or entire sections that you have sweated over. Many good writers are really just good editors. They have learned to look at their first draft with a critical eye and make it better.

Inexperienced writers are more likely to do too little self-editing than too much. The main problem isn't usually too little time; it's that they are insufficiently ruthless. There is probably no more famous writing advice than that of Sir Arthur Quiller-Couch, a literary critic: "Whenever you feel an impulse to perpetrate a piece of exceptionally fine writing, obey it—wholeheartedly—and delete it before sending your manuscript to press. Murder your darlings."

Writers become attached to the words they have produced with so much toil. The problem is the sunk-cost fallacy: the error of continuing down the wrong path because you cannot bear to accept that the work done was wasted. One way to avoid this is to get a first draft down quickly, before sitting down to polish. This way, beautiful sentences emerge later in the process, and don't need to be killed.

Your biggest aid is time. If you have some, set your first draft aside for a while before you settle down to edit. Even one night's sleep is better than nothing.

At this stage, your aim is to decide whether your piece does what it was supposed to do. Go back to the beginning and see if you have made the points you planned to. Creating a "reverse outline" (pulling the main points from each paragraph and lining them up) can help you spot flaws in structure, like an incomplete argument that either needs filling out (if kept) or filleting out (if a distraction).

Once you're sure that your structure works, try to read your story aloud. This slows you down and makes your words less familiar. You will be less likely to skim over clunky phrasing, or words you accidentally repeated or omitted. You might notice that you skipped steps in an argument. Make a note of anywhere that you hesitate or stumble: this often indicates an awkward transition or missing signposting.

If you can, get someone else to read your work. Explain that you're not looking for a proofreader: what you want is someone who will note when they lose the thread or find something confusing or laboured. Ask them what they think your main point was. With luck, it will be what you intended.

If another reader isn't available, try a thought experiment. Imagine you are asked to write a second, related piece: perhaps, in *Economist* terms, a leader that uses your original story as the reporting upon which it is based. What would it say? Now ask yourself whether someone reading your original would be able to predict this—and whether you want them to be able to.

If your original story aimed to persuade, or make a recommendation, then your editorial should match this purpose. If it does not, then your original may not have made the case you intended.

If your piece was limited to exposition, ask yourself what a leader based on it would say. This is a way of revealing what you actually think, now that you have done all the research, reporting and writing.

You can then ask whether your opinions are visible in what you wrote, and whether they should be.

Simplify, then exaggerate

Once the pieces are in place, the next step is line-editing (or copy-editing)—improving your sentences and words.

The motto of *The Economist* is sometimes said jokingly to be "simplify, then exaggerate." It is right and proper to be clear about caveats and uncertainty; it is quite another thing to distance yourself from your own words. Some writers, without intending to, habitually shift to softenings, evasions and passives whenever they say something striking, definite or controversial.

If you are sure a statement is right, and that you have provided the evidence, stand by it. In other words, as you edit, cut every *arguably*, *some say* or *it might be the case* that you can. Is your reader a hostile lawyer who will pick apart the slightest inaccuracy? In that case, include the necessary hedges. But if you can assume your reader is charitable, then for the most part dispense with *for the most part*; such phrases slow down your writing and sap it of energy.

You should be scrupulous in giving arguments you disagree with their fair weight. Constructing a "steel man", the strongest possible case against yourself that you can summon, is far more persuasive than debating a straw man. You should cite the most persuasive opponents of your argument that you can find.

But you should also avoid false balance—suggesting that there are two sides to the story when one of those sides has much more going for it. Avoid vacillating between the options, or sitting on the fence between them. Set out the various cases with the greatest force you can, and let the weight of evidence fall where it may.

See if you can cut *rather*, *somewhat*, *possibly*, *mostly*, *actually*, *really* and so on.

Very is a special case. Though it looks like an intensifier, it weakens what it modifies. Saying *He is an honest man* is a categorical statement. *He is a very honest man* puts the subject on a scale of honesty near the top, but leaves room for improvement. Try cutting *very*.

And *quite* is dangerous: it is always an intensifier in American

English but can mean *somewhat* in British English, and so damn with faint praise.

Pacing

If you are Proust, then feel free to write tens of thousands of words about loss and memory; the rest of us are best off writing as crisply as we can. That said, whenever you simply have to explain something complicated, give your reader fair warning and slow down. The aim isn't to maintain an even pace. It is to gallop along when the way is clear and take your time when the going is treacherous. At such points add extra signposting and support: a reminder of what you are about to cover, with examples and metaphors.

This is also a good moment to look at the "furniture" on your pages. A wall of uninterrupted text is intimidating. So if you haven't already, think about where it can be broken up with cross-heads (also known as sub-heads), and what charts or tables will do the work of elucidating. Look for over-long paragraphs, and break them up so that each lays out one idea. "The paragraph", said Fowler, "is essentially a unit of thought, not of length; it must be homogeneous in subject matter and sequential in treatment."

One-sentence paragraphs should be used only occasionally.

Have you struck the right path between insulting your audience by explaining the obvious, and abandoning them by assuming too much knowledge? It is not really until you have a first draft that you can tell where you have rushed and where you have dragged. Perhaps you have added some tiresome material for reference, which slows things down and risks causing your reader to lose the thread. Instead, imagine you're a hard-boiled fiction editor asking a novelist how the purple passage about the sunset moves the story forward. Everything should serve your goal.

Active, crisp and concrete

Is your tone warm but professional, neither casual nor stuffy? Are most of your sentences on the short side, but not to the extent that the rhythm is staccato or monotonous? Do most sentences, especially the long ones, have the actor and action near their start? Do your sentences hand off well, one to the next?

Does your document brim with real people doing concrete things, rather than abstract nouns undergoing disembodied phenomena? Check specifically for nominalisations—those abstract nouns (covered in Chapter 2) such as *expansion, investigation, contraction, observation* and *variation* that pair with boring verbs (*to be, to have, to become, to seem*). If you move the action into the verb, your writing will become livelier and, as a bonus for when you come to trimming your piece, shorter, too.

If you are writing about abstractions such as company profits or the state of the economy, you may feel absolved from this advice to write about real people doing concrete things. But even then, remember why you write about these abstractions: because they affect real customers, suppliers and workers as they buy, sell and labour. That impact should be clear and forceful in your words.

Now is the moment to be brutal with any remaining acronyms, buzzwords, jargon and dead metaphors. Good writers work hard to avoid whichever expressions are all the rage in meetings (*deep dive; move the needle; build back better*). Have you instead used crisp and fresh words, apt and original figures of speech, and clear, informative examples and illustrations?

This is also a good point to edit out any personal tics. Only when you read your document as a whole can you see if you are overly fond of *actually* or *thus*. If you find lots of things *fascinating* or *compelling*, that's good—but find some synonyms too. Finally, see if you reach too often for semicolons, dashes, colons and other tricks instead of the sturdy full stop.

Tightening up

After you have the structure in place and have improved things sentence by sentence, now is the time to tighten everything up. Scan for adjectives and adverbs that are entirely unnecessary—such as the *entirely* in this sentence. Or you may find one word that does the work of two (*sprinting* for *running swiftly*). The aim isn't to get rid of all adjectives or adverbs. But you should decide whether each word is earning its keep.

The phrases *there is* and *there are* are weak. Turn *there was a 23% increase in sales* into *sales increased by 23%*.

Look for constructions phrased negatively (*It is not easy to tell*; *It does not happen often*). Often, these can be replaced by positive versions (*It is hard to tell*; *It happens rarely*). These are shorter and more definite.

Moreover, as negative statements pile up, it is easy to lose track of how many you have used, and to end up saying the opposite of what you meant. Try to parse the likes of "*That doesn't mean we don't think there aren't things that can be improved*", and see if it means what it purports to. Those writers who *never fail to neglect eliminating* such constructions, even when they are correct, leave readers scratching their heads. And replacing two negatives with a positive saves space too.

Trim pleonasms, the use of more words than necessary to get your message across: *rise up, serious crisis, pilotless drone, HIV virus, disappear from sight, free gift, fellow countrymen* and the like (see Redundancy on pp.33-4 for more). All are at least one word too long, because one word in the phrase entails the other. This frees up space for words that add something. And look out for extra prepositions: *freed up, headed up by, bought up, sold off* and *met with* mean *freed, headed by, bought, sold* and *met*.

Watch out for over-abundant superlatives. The most frequent ten buzzwords in press releases, according to one study, are *leader, leading, best, top, unique, great, solution, largest, innovative* and *innovator*. The problem should be obvious. Not everyone can be a leader, the best, the top, the largest and so on. But nearly everyone says they are, making such statements meaningless. Cut these words and let the facts do the work.

Many grammatical words can be cut: *The man who was hit by the trolley* is *The man hit by the trolley*. *He said that he could trim no more* is *He said he could trim no more*. But sometimes such cuts introduce confusion (see Avoiding ambiguity, pp. 41-2). Make sure they do not: a sentence that is clear to the writer (who knows all the underlying facts) may not be to the reader.

Having done all this, you may have painlessly cut your draft to a reasonable length. Congratulations—now you have space to restore a telling detail or amusing quote that didn't fit before.

Then proofread

Print out your document if you can. Most people see mistakes more easily on paper than on a screen. Mark any changes on the printout, then correct the digital version.

Don't rely entirely on a spelling and grammar checker, but do use one. Those in the major word-processing packages both miss some genuine errors and flag some false ones. But they are good at spotting typos and mismatches between singular subjects and plural verbs (*The problems...is*). You should still search for further typos yourself, especially those that are real words and therefore more likely to be missed by computer programs: *on* for *or*; *it* for *is* or *pubic* for *public*.

Don't forget to proofread headings, sub-headings and any captions.

In summary, "The best way to be boring is to leave nothing out" (Voltaire). Read through what you have written several times, editing it mercilessly, whether by trimming, polishing or sharpening. Cut out anything repetitive or superfluous. What Raymond Mortimer said of Susan Sontag is true of most writers: "Her journalism, like a diamond, will sparkle more if it is cut."

part 2

The details

6

Confusables and cuttables: individual rulings

This chapter contains rulings on individual words, organised alphabetically. Words that are commonly misused, or confused with other words, are listed here. But the rulings below also include many words widely used in loose or extended senses, but which *The Economist* uses only in older senses; these are best considered matters of style, not strict correctness, and the wordings of these rulings should make clear which is which. Finally, the "cuttables" promised in the chapter title are those words that are best excised from your writing and replaced with something else.

absent

Use as an adjective (*their friends were absent*) or, if you must, a verb (*he absented himself*). But the preposition (*absent new evidence, the jury must acquit*) is an Americanism. Use *without, in the absence of*, etc.

acronym

Strictly, this is a pronounceable word formed from the initials of other words, like *radar*, NIMBY or NATO. A set of capitals like the BBC or the IMF make up an *initialism*.

actionable

This word means *giving ground for a lawsuit*. Do not use it to mean capable of being put into practice: prefer *practical* or *practicable*.

address

By all means *address an audience* or a *letter*, but this word is overused. Questions can be *answered*, issues *discussed*, problems *solved*, difficulties *dealt with*.

adjectives of proper nouns

If proper nouns have adjectives, use them. The Crimea war? The Spain Inquisition? The Russia revolution? "The France Connection"? No: the Crimean war, the Spanish Inquisition, the Russian revolution, "The French Connection". So also the *Pakistani* (not *Pakistan*) government, the *Lebanese* (not *Lebanon*) civil war, the *Mexican* (not *Mexico*) problem, etc.

It is permissible to use the noun as an adjective if to do otherwise would cause confusion: an *African initiative* suggests the proposal came from Africa, whereas an *Africa initiative* suggests it was about Africa.

In the case of American places, where the adjective is common and feels natural, use it, especially when describing properties or culture: *a Texan tradition, Californian cuisine*. But in many cases this simply looks too odd for the people who live there, who after all have *Texas Rangers* and *California dreaming*. In politics, this will typically be the case: an *Arkansas* (not *Arkansan*) Senate race.

adjective placement

Be careful when using adjectives for explanation. To write *Germany's liberal Free Democrats* can imply not that Germany's Free Democrats are liberals, as intended, but that this is a subgroup to be distinguished from the illiberal Free Democrats. Similarly, *China's southern Guangdong province* suggests that the place under discussion is the southern Guangdong province, not the northern one. Try *the Free Democrats, Germany's liberal party* or *Guangdong province, in southern China*.

administration

Use of *administration* to mean a country's political leadership should be reserved for those with presidential systems, especially America's.

Parliamentary systems have *governments*, and *administration* can refer to the permanent civil service.

advertisement, ad

Avoid *advert*. If you must shorten *advertisement*, go for *ad*.

aetiology

Aetiology is the science of causation, or an inquiry into something's origins, and spelt thus in British English.

affect, effect

To *affect* means to influence or have an impact on someone or something, or in other words, produce an *effect*.

A different verb, *to affect*, means to put on a false show of something, as in *to affect an upper-class accent*.

Confusingly, *effect* is also a verb, meaning to bring something about.

And *affect* is also a noun, with its stress on the first syllable, meaning someone's feelings and emotions, especially as manifested by their appearance, as in *a flat affect*.

(See also **effectively**, **in effect** and **effectual**.)

affordable

By whom? Avoid *affordable housing*, *affordable computers* and the like when you mean something is *subsidised*, *inexpensive* or merely *cheap*.

aggravate

Use it when you mean to *worsen*, not as a synonym for *irritate* or *annoy*.

aggression

Aggression is an unattractive quality, so do not call a *keen* salesman an *aggressive* one (unless his foot is in the door).

agree

Use with prepositions: things are *agreed on, to* or *about*, not just *agreed*.

alibi

An *alibi* is the fact of being elsewhere as a legal defence. It is not the same thing as a false explanation (though an alibi offered may well be false).

alternate, alternative

Alternate, as an adjective, means *every other* (*He showers on alternate days*). As a noun, it means a *stand-in*.

As an adjective, *alternative* means *of two or more things*, or *possible as an alternative* (eg, *They were offered alternative jobs*).

among

Not *amongst*.

an

An should be used before a word beginning with a vowel sound (*an egg, an umbrella, an MP*) or an *h* if the *h* is silent (*an honorary degree*). But *a European, a university, a hospital, a hotel. Historical, historic* and *historian* are preceded by *a*.

analogue, homologue

An *analogue* is of *similar function* to something else. A *homologue corresponds in its nature* to something else (as a bird's wing and a seal's flipper do to a human arm) because of common evolutionary origin.

anarchy

Anarchy means the complete absence of law or government. It may be harmonious or chaotic.

animals

For the spelling of the names of animals, plants, etc, see **Latin names**.

annus horribilis

This is used, in contrast to *annus mirabilis*, to describe an awful year. It serves its purpose, but it should be noted that *annus mirabilis* originally meant much the same thing: 1666, of which it was first used, was the year of the great fire of London and the second year of the great plague in England. Physicists, though, have used *annus mirabilis* to describe 1932, the year in which the neutron was discovered, the positron identified and the atomic nucleus first broken up artificially.

anon

Anon means *soon*.

anticipate

Do not use *anticipate* for the simpler *expect*. Use *anticipate* to mean doing something ahead of something else (eg, to forestall an undesired consequence), as in *They anticipated the attack, setting up minefields and anti-tank equipment.*

apostasy, heresy, blasphemy

If you abandon your religion, you commit *apostasy*. If that religion is the prevailing one in your community, and your beliefs are contrary to its orthodoxy, you commit *heresy*. Speech deemed offensively irreverent of deities and cherished religious beliefs is *blasphemy*.

appeal

Appeal is intransitive (except in America), so *appeal against* decisions.

appraise, apprise

Appraise means *set a price on*. *Apprise* means *inform*.

arrant, errant

The two are etymological cousins, but with distinct meanings.
Arrant means *downright* or *unmitigated*. *Errant* meaning *wandering*,
off-course or *wide of the mark*. *"Errant nonsense"* is therefore incorrect
in its intended use, though it may be an unintentionally good self-
description.

assassinate

Assassinate is, properly, the term used not just for any old killing, but
for the murder of a prominent person, usually for a political purpose.
See **execute**.

autarchy, autarky

Autarchy means absolute sovereignty. *Autarky* means self-sufficiency.

avert, avoid, evade

To *avert something* means to *head it off*. To *avoid* it means to *keep away
from it*. To *evade it* means to *elude it* or *escape it artfully*. Note that *tax
avoidance* is legal; *tax evasion* is not.

avocation

An *avocation* is a *diversion from your ordinary employment*, or even a
hobby, not a synonym for *vocation*.

bail, bale

Bale in a hayfield, but *bail* from jail, or with a pail. The second of
these comes from a word for "authority" or "custody" and is related
to *bailiff*. The third, to empty a boat of water, is the source of most of
the metaphorical uses. Hence to *bail out* (someone or a company in
difficulty).

-based

A *Paris-based group* may be all right, if, say, that group operates in
several countries (otherwise just say a *group in Paris*). But avoid

community-based, faith-based, knowledge-based, etc. A *community-based organisation* is perhaps a *community organisation*. A *faith-based organisation* is probably a *religious charity*. A *knowledge-based industry* needs explanation: all industries depend on knowledge.

beg the question

Do not use *beg the question* for *raise the question* or *evade the answer*. To beg the question is to adopt an argument whose validity depends upon assuming the truth of the very conclusion the argument is designed to produce. (See also Borrowing specialist terms, pp. 30-32.)

bellwether

Note the spelling. A *bellwether* is the leading sheep of a flock, on whose neck a bell is hung, from *wether*, a male sheep. It has nothing to do with prevailing winds.

between

Some insist that, where division is involved, *among* should be used where three or more are concerned, *between* where only two are concerned. This distinction is unnecessary. But take care with *between*. To *fall between two stools*, however painful, is grammatically acceptable; to *fall between the cracks* is to challenge the laws of physics.

biannual, biennial, biweekly, bimonthly, bicentennial

Biannual can mean twice a year or once every two years. Avoid. Since *biennial* also means once every two years, that is best avoided too. *Bimonthly* and *biweekly* are similarly ambiguous. Fortunately *fortnightly* is not.

For the noun meaning a 200th anniversary, use *bicentenary*. For the adjective, *bicentennial*.

black

In the black means *in profit*, in contrast to *in the red*. But it can also be misunderstood. Avoid.

blond, blonde

Blond, like some other English nouns, has both a masculine and a feminine form. Unlike most of these nouns, however, blond is also an adjective and, unusually, in its adjectival use it retains its two genders. Use *blonde* to describe fair-haired women, and *blond* for everything else, including the hair of a blonde.

blooded, bloodied

Blooded can mean *pedigreed*, or also *initiated* (from the practice of smearing the face of a hunter with the blood of a first kill). *Bloodied* means *wounded*.

blue and red

Be careful in political context. American usage (*red* for Republican, *blue* for Democratic) is the opposite of almost everyone else's, where *red* is *left-wing*.

bon vivant

Bon vivant, not *bon viveur*.

both...and

A preposition placed after *both* should be repeated after *and*. Thus, *both to the right and to the left*. (See Parallelism, p. 46.)

bowdlerisation

Thomas Bowdler's version of Shakespeare, produced in 1818 using "judicious" paraphrase and expurgation, was designed to be read by men to their families with no one offended or embarrassed. In doing so, he gave his name to an insidious form of censorship. Use the word, but avoid the practice of *bowdlerisation* in your own writing.

brokerage

Brokerage is what a stockbroking firm does, not what it is.

by contrast, in contrast

Use *by contrast* only when comparing one thing with another: *Somalia is a poor country. By contrast, Egypt is rich.* This means Egypt is rich by comparison with Somalia, though by other standards it may be poor. If you are simply noting a difference, say *in contrast: David Cameron, like Tony Blair, likes to spend his holidays in Tuscany. In contrast, Gordon Brown used to go to Kirkcaldy.* In contrast *to*, not *with*.

Canute

When King *Canute* ordered the tide to cease, he did so to prove to flattering courtiers that he had no such power and that it would come anyway. If using him as a byword, it should be for humility. Don't imply he was surprised to get his feet wet.

career, careen

As a verb, *career* means to *gallop* or *rush*. (The noun *career* means the rush through life, or the part of it that passes as a job.) *Careen* means to turn a boat on its side (particularly to clean or repair its hull).

cartel

A *cartel* is a group that controls supply in order to drive up prices. Do not use it to describe any old syndicate or association of producers—especially of drugs—unless they engage in cartel behaviour.

case

"There is perhaps no single word so freely resorted to as a trouble-saver," says Gowers, "and consequently responsible for so much flabby writing." Often you can do without it. *There are many cases of it being unnecessary* is better as *It is often unnecessary. As is always the case when* means *As always when. If it is the case that* simply means *If. It is not the case* means *It is not so.*

Cassandra

Do not use *Cassandra* as a synonym for any prophet of doom. Her curse was that her predictions were always correct, but never believed.

catalyst

This is something that speeds up a chemical reaction while itself remaining unchanged. Do not confuse it with one of the agents.

celibacy, chastity, abstinence

Celibate originally meant *unmarried*. *Chaste* meant not taking part in unlawful sex (but that could mean having sex only within marriage). Times have rendered *chastity* rare (and often misunderstood to mean *abstinence* only), and *celibacy* is now also understood to mean *abstinence*. When writing about these, use context to be clear.

centred

Centred *on*, not *around* or *in*.

challenge

Modern life seems to consist of little else but *challenges*. At every turn, every president, every minister, every government, every business, everyone everywhere is faced with them. No one has to face a *change*, *difficulty*, *task* or *job*. Next time you face a *challenge* on the page, challenge yourself to find a more specific, less overused word.

charge

If you *charge* intransitively, do so as a bull, cavalry officer or the like, not as an accuser. In other words, avoid *The writing was abysmal, he charged*, which should have a direct object: *He charged his trainees with abysmal writing*. (See **transitive and intransitive verbs** later in this chapter.)

check, cheque, chequer

As a verb, *check* means *bring to a halt* or to *ascertain the accuracy of something*. As a noun, it means, a *stop* or *rebuff*, or a position in chess, or a *square*, as on a tablecloth. A *cheque* is an *order for money*. A *chequer* is a pattern of different-coloured squares. So *chequered* means eventful or variegated, as in the euphemism of a *chequered past*.

cherry-pick

If you must use this cliché, note that to *cherry-pick* means to engage in careful rather than indiscriminate selection. A *cherry-picker* is a machine for raising pickers (and cleaners and so on) off the ground.

circumstances

Circumstances stand around a thing, so it is *in*, not *under*, them.

civil society

Civil society pops up a lot these days, often in the similarly vague company of *community leaders*, *good governance*, *the international community*, *social capital* and the like. It can, however, be a useful term to describe collectively all non-commercial organisations between the family and the state. Do not use it as a synonym for NGOs (non-governmental organisations), which is how it is usually loosely employed.

co-

The prefix *co-* is redundant in sentences like *He co-founded the company with Sir Alan* or *He co-wrote "The Left Nation" with Adrian Wulfric*. But *co-wrote* is fine if the other *co-author* is not mentioned. Do not *co-author* (or even *author*) as a verb, though. And avoid neologisms like *co-sleeping*.

coiffed

Coiffed, not *coiffured*.

collectable

Since almost anything can be collected, *collectable* tells the reader little. *Valuable*, *popular* or *in demand* is probably what you mean.

come up with

Try *suggest*, *originate* or *produce*.

community

Community is useful when referring to people actually acting in communion. A community (whether a town, ethnic group or religion) may pull together after a tragedy, for example. In other cases (see Respect and clarity, pp. 34-5) you may be implying a unity that does not exist. And in other uses, the word is empty.

The *business community* means *businessmen* (who are supposed to be competing, not colluding). The *intelligence community*, though a particularly common usage in America, usually means *spies* (and indeed the intelligence community's failure to act like one is often responsible for intelligence failures). The *development community* probably means NGOs. The *international community*, if it means anything, means *other countries, aid agencies* or, just occasionally, *the family of nations*. The members of the *global community* are a mystery. The *criminal community*, mentioned in a letter to the *Financial Times* (March 22nd 2013), may well have a sense of brotherhood. Whether the same can be said of the *tornado community*, cited by an assistant professor of meteorology and climatology at Mississippi State University, is another matter.

compare to, compare with

A traditional rule has it that *compared to* is for a simple likeness (*He compared his brother to Groucho Marx*), while *compared with* is used to evaluate similarities and highlight differences too (*Compared with Ronald Reagan, George H.W. Bush, though a principled conservative, was seen as squishy on policy and wooden in salesmanship.*)

The distinction is worth observing. But some comparisons both liken and draw distinctions, as in the famous case of *"Shall I compare thee to a summer's day?"* The answer given by the poet is both "yes" and "no": his subject is "more fair and more temperate" and, unlike a summer day, will not fade. In such cases, either would work.

compensation

Try to reserve *compensation* for amends, especially for a loss. Workers get *wages, salary* or simply *pay*, and a lucky few get *bonuses*. If you must, stock options and the like can be included in *compensation* too, but best to spell out what you mean.

compound

Do not use *compound* where the more straightforward *worsen* or even just *increase* would do.

comprise

Comprise is contaminated. Originally, *a whole comprised the parts* (as in *the European Union comprises 27 countries*). But in the 18th century people began using it the other way round, writing that the *parts comprised the whole*. It was a short step to the ubiquitous but much-deprecated *the whole is comprised of the parts*, probably via confusion with *is composed of*.

If you write *the EU comprises 27 countries* you will confuse some readers, and if you write *the EU is comprised of 27 countries* you will annoy others. *Consists of* and *is composed of* are less likely to trip you up.

The mess arises because the Latin roots of *comprise* are not transparent to most people. That's why an old Anglo-Saxonism (see Chapter 1) can save you: *make up* or *is made up of* is best.

contemporary

Means *at that same time*, so when writing about the past, *contemporary prices* are not today's.

continual, continuous

Continuous describes something uninterrupted. *Continual* admits of a break. If your neighbours play loud music every night, it is a *continual* nuisance. It is not a *continuous* one unless the music is never turned off.

convince

Do not *convince people to do something* or to believe something. The verb you want is *persuade*. *The prime minister was persuaded [by others] to call a June election; he was convinced of the wisdom of doing so only after he had won.*

core

Like *key*, *core* is used too often as a trendy modifier. Do not write *This is the core problem*.

coruscate

This means *sparkle* or *throw off flashes of light*, not *devastate* or *lash* (that's *excoriate*) or reduce to wrinkles (that's *corrugate*). Neither does *coruscating* mean *corrosive*, *bitter* or *burning* (that's *caustic*).

cost-effective

Cost-effective sounds authoritative, but *does it mean good value, gives a big bang for the buck* or just plain *cheap*? If cheap, say cheap.

could

Could is useful as a variant of *may* or *might*: *His coalition could (may or might) collapse*. But take care. Does *He could call an election in June* mean *He may call an election in June* or *He would be allowed to call an election in June*?

In general, prefer *may*, which is usually more precise. Why? Take a headline like *"Chairman could have embezzled millions"*, which could mean he was in a position to do so (but did not) or that he *may have*. See **may, might** on p. 54.

crescendo

This is a *passage of increasing loudness*. Do not use as a synonym for *peak* or *zenith*, and therefore do not *build to a crescendo*.

crisis

A *crisis* is a *decisive event* or *turning-point* (as its relation to *critical* suggests). Avoid over-use or exaggeration. Not everything is a crisis. Many of the economic and political conditions described as *crises* are really *persistent troubles* which, though unpleasant, can be borne for a long time.

critique

Prefer to *offer a critique* or similar rather than verbing *critique*, though *to critique* is permissible if alternatives do not work. It is not the same as *to criticise*, which is to offer a negative appraisal rather than a thoughtful one.

current

Somewhat like *contemporary*, *current* can mean *at that time* (*the rumour was current that the president was corrupt*), but is also loosely used to mean *relating to today*. To avoid confusion, use *today's prices*, etc, when writing about the present.

data

Data was originally plural in English; the singular was *datum*, from Latin. But few speak of *a datum* any more (it is *a piece of data*). And the world is so filled with data that most people don't think of individual data points; they think of a mass of information. So *data*, like *agenda*, *candelabra* and *stamina* before it, has gone from being a classical plural to an English singular for many speakers. Indeed, the singular has overtaken the plural in prevalence.

The existence of the uncontroversial *piece of data* makes plain that even sticklers for the old form can conceive of data as singular: *a piece of* goes only with singular nouns, like *a piece of popcorn*, *a piece of pie*. It cannot be used with plurals like *a piece of raisins*, *a piece of cupcakes*.

Use the plural when you are talking about collected observations (*Data from NOAA's weather stations indicate that...*). But use the singular when you are speaking either about the concept (*Data is the new oil*, *Data is more important than physical inventory*), or the totality (*the data held by Google is equivalent to a stack of printed paper reaching the Moon*).

deal

Do not *deal* drugs, horses, weapons, etc; *deal in* them.

decimate

Use *decimate* to mean to destroy a significant proportion of something. Use *annihilate*, *wipe out* or something else for utter destruction.

degrees

Universities give *degrees*. American high schools award *diplomas*.

deprecate, depreciate

To *deprecate* is to argue or plead against, and therefore to run down or belittle something. To *depreciate* is to fall in value.

different

Use *different from*, not the British alternative *different to* or the American *different than*.

dilemma

Do not use for any old awkwardness. The original *dilemma* was an argument offering an adversary two choices (the *horns* of the dilemma), both unfavourable. A dilemma thus offers a choice of between alternatives with equally nasty consequences.

disconnect

This voguish nouning of the verb *to disconnect* implies that a connection made in the past is now severed, as in an interrupted call. However, the person who reaches for *disconnect*—more often *total disconnect*—usually wants to use it to describe not the breaking but the absence of any connection: *The San Francisco Fed's economic projections show a total disconnect from the real world.* This would be better as *The San Francisco Fed's economic projections have no connection with the real world.*

discreet, discrete

Discreet means circumspect or prudent; *discrete* means separate or distinct. Remember, "Questions are never indiscreet. Answers sometimes are." (Oscar Wilde)

disinterested, uninterested

Disinterested means impartial; *uninterested* means bored. "Disinterested curiosity is the lifeblood of civilisation." (G.M. Trevelyan)

dived

For the past tense and past participle of *dive*, use *dived*, not *dove* (see Chapter 10 on British-American distinctions like this).

down to

Down to earth, yes, but *Occasional court victories are not down to human rights* (*The Economist*)? Use *caused by, attributable to, the responsibility of* or *explained by*.

driver

Once familiar behind steering wheels, *drivers*—often *key drivers*—are now behind change of every kind, as in "Women are the drivers of positive change." Try *agent* for a human. If speaking of a force, as in *the key driver of growth in the fourth quarter*, try *source* or *cause*.

due process

Due process is a technical term which may not be understood by non-Americans, even though it was first used in England in 1355. It comes in two forms, *substantive due process*, which relates to the duties of governments to act rationally and proportionally when doing anything that affects citizens' rights, and *procedural due process*, which relates to the need for fair procedures. If you use the expression, make sure it is clear what you mean by it. A preferable alternative may be *legally, properly* or *in accordance with the law*.

due to

Due to modifies a noun, because *due* is an adjective. So you can write *The cancellation, due to rain, of...* Though it is now often used like an adverb, modifying a verb (*It was cancelled due to rain*), *because of*, *on account of* and *owing to* are better.

effectively, in effect, effectual

Use *effectively* to mean *with effect*, usually a positive effect: *The prime minister dealt with the latest crisis effectively.*

If you mean *in effect*, say that: *Owing to inflation, the 2% pay increase was in effect a 1% pay cut*, not *was effectively a 1% pay cut.*

Effectual means *carried out with the intended effect*, as in *The emergency measures were effectual.*

elite

Once meaning a *chosen group* or *the pick of the bunch*, *elite* is now almost always used pejoratively. It is commonplace to say voters are sick of elites, but of whom exactly? *The rich? Globe-trotting executives? Politicians? Academics? Actors* or *cultural taste-makers?* Writing about populism often means writing about voters who are not quite sure whom to be angry with. But you should be more specific. Do not use *elites* as an unspecified boo-word.

enclave, exclave

An *enclave* is a piece of territory entirely surrounded by foreign territory (Lesotho, Nagorno-Karabakh, etc). An *exclave* belongs to but is separated from another country, like Russia's Kaliningrad or Spain's Ceuta and Melilla. Some places might be both. If you are focused on the territory's isolation, *enclave* would work. If your focus is on the mainland country, *exclave* is better.

endemic, epidemic, pandemic

Endemic means prevalent or generally found in a place or population: *Malaria is endemic in some tropical climates.* An *epidemic* means prevalent among a population at a particular time: *America's opioid epidemic takes thousands of lives each year. Pandemic* is used for a global outbreak of disease like covid-19.

enormity

Enormity traditionally means a *crime* or *monstrous wickedness*. For the great size of something, use *magnitude*: *The magnitude of his misdeeds became clear only after his death.*

environment

Often cuttable, as in *the business environment, the work environment,* etc. Try to rephrase—*conditions for business, at work,* etc. *Surroundings* can sometimes do the job.

epicentre

Epicentre means that point on the surface (usually the Earth's) above the centre of something below (usually an earthquake). This can be extended metaphorically to mean the centre of some other great upheaval or disaster, but do not use it as a fancy synonym for *centre*.

The *hypocentre*, in contrast, is the place on the surface (usually of the Earth) below something above (usually an explosion).

eponymous

This is the adjective of *eponym*, which is the person or thing after which something is named. So Hellen was the *eponymous ancestor* of the Hellenes, Ninus was the *eponymous founder* of Nineveh and the fourth Earl of Sandwich was the *eponymous inventor* of the sandwich. Although many others do, do not say *John Sainsbury, the founder of the eponymous supermarket,* but *of the supermarket bearing his name.*

ethnic and racial groups

In general, use the words that people would describe themselves with in ordinary conversation.

People of colour is awkward and to be avoided, as it lumps together highly distinct groups. It is basically a synonym for *non-white*. This defines people as what they are not, but can nonetheless be best when reporting on disparities in majority-white countries, when lacking the privileges of the majority is exactly what is at issue.

In America, prefer *black* to *African-American*, though the latter is still in circulation.

With indigenous peoples, it is better to speak of specific tribal groups where possible. When speaking about the overall population, most indigenous Australians should be called *Aboriginal people* (with upper case, and not *Aborigines* or *Aboriginals*), with the adjective *Aboriginal*. But this term does not include *Torres Strait Islanders*.

In Canada the groups include the *First Nations*, *Métis* and *Inuit*. Avoid *Eskimo*, a name given by outsiders, even if some groups still use it. And certainly avoid the cliché about words for snow.

In the United States both *Native American* and *Indian* are acceptable. But to avoid confusion with people from India, use *Native Americans* on first mention and *Indians* or *Native Americans* fairly interchangeably in later references.

When writing about Spanish-speaking people and their descendants in the United States, use either *Latino* or *Hispanic* as a general term, but try to be specific (eg, *Mexican-American*). Note that many Latin Americans (eg, those from Brazil) are not *Hispanic*.

In Britain, *Asian* is primarily used to mean immigrants and their descendants from the Indian subcontinent. Many are coming to dislike the term, and foreigners may assume it means people from all over Asia, so take care.

Africans may be descended from Asians, Europeans or black Africans. If you specifically mean the latter, write *black Africans*.

In South Africa, *Afrikaners* are whites descended primarily from Dutch immigrants who speak *Afrikaans*—a language descended from Dutch but distinct. People of mixed race in South Africa are *Coloureds* (many of whom also speak Afrikaans).

Despite the popularity of the term in other languages, *Anglo-Saxon* is not a synonym for *English-speaking*, nor even for *British*. *Anglo-Saxon capitalism* does not exist.

Call the language spoken in Iran *Persian* (not *Farsi*).

Flemings speak *Dutch* (not *Flemish*).

Ethnic, meaning concerning nations or races or even something ill-defined in between, can be a useful word. But do not be shy of *race* and *racial* where that is the most precise word. American Latinos are considered an ethnicity that can be of any race. Black Americans are generally seen to share a race despite coming from many different ethnicities.

euthanasia, euthanise

Euthanasia is *assisted dying*, a better term, though *euthanasia* may be used for variation. But avoid the verb *euthanise*. Animals may be *put to sleep*. Humans are *helped to die* (or use a more specific description, as appropriate).

evangelical, evangelistic

Evangelical means pertaining to the *Gospel* and so, among Protestants, relating to a church that believes in the sole authority and inerrancy of the Bible. Only a church with *Evangelical* in its name, or a member of such a church, should be given an initial capital; the rest are *evangelical*.

Evangelistic means prone to evangelising, which is to say preaching, though not necessarily religiously.

ex-

Ex- (and *former*): be careful. A *communist ex-member* has lost his seat; an *ex-communist member* has lost his party.

exception that proves the rule

This proverb derives from an old legal maxim: *The exception confirms the rule in cases not excepted.* For example, in *No parking on Sundays*, the ban on Sundays implicitly confirms a rule allowing parking on other days.

Do not use this to mean *the existence of an exception affirms the validity of the rule*.

execute

Execute means *put to death by law*. Do not use it as a synonym for *murder*. An *extra-judicial execution* is a contradiction in terms. (See also **assassinate**.)

exhausting, exhaustive

One is *tiring*, the other *thorough*.

existential

Existential means *of or pertaining to existence*. In logic it may mean predicating existence. It is sometimes used in such phrases as *existential threat or existential crisis*, where the author wants it to mean a threat to the existence (of Israel, say) or a crisis that calls into question the purpose of something's existence (eg, NATO). Do not use to mean merely *grave* or *serious*.

experience

By all means accumulate experience, and even experiences, but avoid them in your prose in phrases like *user experience, customer experience* and *dining experience*.

factoid

This is originally something that is thought by many to be a fact, but is not in fact a fact. The -oid suffix ("having the form of") is the key: a *spheroid* is not quite a *sphere*, and the *deltoid* muscle is only roughly shaped like the Greek letter *delta*. If you mean *an amusing fact*, say that. If you mean an *urban legend*, that would be clearer than *factoid*.

fed up

Fed up with, not *of*. Ditto, *bored*.

fellow

Perfectly good as a stand-alone noun, but unnecessary before *countrymen*, *classmates* and other nouns that already imply fellow status: "Friends, Romans, fellow countrymen"?

feral

This word can mean brutish or uncultivated, but is best used of plants, animals, children, etc, that were once tamed or domesticated but have run wild.

ferment, foment

These are two unrelated words that can sometimes, as transitive verbs, be used interchangeably. To *ferment* means to *cause fermentation*, to *agitate*, to *excite*—or indeed to *foment*, which means to foster, stimulate or instigate (trouble, usually).

fewer than, less than

Use *fewer*, not less, with individual items, which can usually be counted: *fewer than seven samurai* (not *less than seven samurai*). *Less* is used for masses: *The pessimist retorted that a glass half empty has no less water than a glass half full.*

Not all numbers need *fewer*. Write *less than £200, less than 700 tonnes of oil, less than a third of Americans*, because these are measured quantities or proportions, not individual items. Time, distance and other things measured on a continuum also take *less; in less than six weeks, less than six feet tall.*

One less before a noun (*boron has one less electron than carbon*) is acceptable. Standing alone, *one fewer* is fine: *He had not 100 problems, but one fewer. One fewer* also precedes *than: the party won 16 seats, one fewer than at the last election.*

fief

Fief, not *fiefdom*.

first, second, third

When enumerating your points use these, not *firstly, secondly, thirdly.*

flatline

Some use this verb to mean *no longer growing*, as in a curve going flat. Others use it to mean *to die*, as when an electrocardiogram reports no heartbeat. These are very different things, good reason enough to avoid this verb (besides the fact that it is also a cliché).

flaunt, flout

Flaunt means *display*; flout means *disdain*. Though both involve a kind of insouciance, if you flout the distinction, you will flaunt your carelessness.

fold

Use *-fold* only for increases, not decreases.

forego, forgo

Forgo means *do without*; it forgoes the *e*. *Forego* means *go before*, as the spelling indicates. A *foregone conclusion* is predetermined; a *forgone conclusion* is non-existent.

forensic

Forensic means *pertaining to courts of law* (held by the Romans in the *forum*) or, more loosely, the *application of science to legal issues*. *Forensic medicine* is *medical jurisprudence*. Do not use *forensic* to mean merely *very detailed*.

former (ex-)

See **ex-**.

former and latter

Avoid the use of *the former* and *the latter* whenever possible. It causes the reader to stop and backtrack, a bad thing.

founder, flounder

If you *flounder*, you struggle clumsily or helplessly. If you *founder*, you stumble (if you're a horse), collapse (a building) or sink (a ship).

Frankenstein

You will probably use him only metaphorically (possibly in a *Frankencliché* like *Frankenfood*). But in case you refer to the novel, *Frankenstein* was not the monster but its creator.

free

Free is an adjective or an adverb, so no need to write *for free*: someone gets something *free* or *for nothing*.

fresh

Fresh is overused journalese for *new* or *more*. *A few hundred fresh bodies are being recovered every day*, reported *The Economist* improbably two months after a tsunami had struck. Use with care.

fulsome

This old word once meant just *copious* or *wholehearted*, usually preceding something like *praise* or *tribute*. But for centuries it has had the taint of *immodest*, *exaggerated* or *insincere* for many people. Avoid, unless context makes absolutely clear which you mean.

gay

When describing someone's sexuality, it is best to use the term they use for themselves: *gay* (adjective only; avoid as a noun); *lesbian*, *bisexual* or *straight*. Gay does not refer just to men—hence *gay marriage*, *gay pride*. Reserve *homosexual* for behaviours and tendencies, not people. Hence a *homosexual liaison* or *homosexual acts*, which could be performed by people who do not see themselves as gay.

gender and sex

The first English meaning of *gender* was grammatical, applied to words, not people. Gender is prominent in languages like Latin or German, where every ordinary noun is masculine, neuter or feminine. This often baffles English-speakers who discover, for example, that the gender of Mädchen, the German word for girl, is neuter.

In the second half of the 20th century gender took on another meaning. Feminists used it to refer to the social and cultural expectations that are built upon sex differences. When people talk about "masculine" or "feminine" behaviour they are talking about gender, not sex. Hence *gender studies*, *gender roles*, *gender bending* and the rest.

Sometimes the right word is simply prescribed by prevailing usage. There is a *gender pay gap* in virtually every country and company (not a *sex pay gap*). Indeed *sex* sometimes clangs if it could be understood to mean sexual intercourse. But do not be afraid of the word when discussing biology.

With job titles, use those generic terms like *police officer* and *firefighter* that have become neutral and natural. It is standard in academia to speak of the *chair of the history department*. But elsewhere *chairman* and *chairwoman* are better. (Avoid *chairpersons*.) With other titles, *actress* and *ballerina* are no more demeaning than *baroness* or *queen*. Use another title only if someone is known to prefer it.

gentlemen's agreement

Gentlemen's agreement, not *gentleman's*.

geography

Geography is the science of the Earth's surface and those who live on it. Do not use it to mean *place* (*She has built a portfolio of directorships in different industries and geographies*). The adjective is *geographical*.

get

Get is an adaptable verb, preferable to *obtain* or *receive* or other Latinisms. But some uses are too breezy: do not *get sacked* or *get promoted*. People *are sacked* or *are promoted*. That also goes for *a prizewinner getting to shake hands with the president*. He *gets the chance to*, or *is allowed to*.

girn, gurn

Use *girn* for *complain*, *gurn* for *pull a face*.

good in parts

Good in parts is what the curate said about an egg that was wholly bad. He was trying to be polite.

gourmet, gourmand

A *gourmet* is a *connoisseur*; a *gourmand* is a *glutton*.

governance, government

Governance has come to mean the system or structure of governing in general. *Government* is the specific instance of this in particular places.

grisly, gristly, grizzly, grizzling

Grisly is frightful. *Gristly* is like school stew. *Grizzly*, a kind of bear, is also an old word for grey, but *grizzled* is better for that purpose. *Grizzling* is grumbling.

halve

Halve is a transitive verb, so deficits, for example, can *double* but should not *halve*. They must *be halved* or *fall by half*.

healthy

Overused (outside medicine and biology). If you think something is *desirable* or *good*, say so. If a company is experiencing good (though not spectacular) profits or growth, try *robust*, *strong* or *impressive*.

heave, heaved, hove

The past participle of *heave* is *heaved*. (The past-tense form *hove* is archaic, or nautical). *To hove* is to *swell*, *rise*, *loiter* or *linger*, but is archaic. Use *hover* or *float*.

heresy

See **apostasy**.

historic, historical

Historic is best reserved for objects, events, eras and so on that may come to be considered *notable in history* (a judgment, incidentally, often made swiftly and implausibly by journalists). *Historical* should be used to mean relating to the past, or to the scholarly study of the past.

hoard, horde

Few secreted treasures (*hoards*) are multitudes on the move (*hordes*).

Hobson's choice

Hobson's choice is not the lesser of two evils. It is take it or leave it, or no choice at all. See **dilemma**.

hoi polloi

Greek for "the many". "Hoi" already means *the*, so classically minded readers see *the hoi polloi* as redundant. But *Hoi polloi were waiting outside* looks bizarre to many others. A good reason to skip this phrase. If you must sneeringly refer to *the masses* (or at the toffs who see the proles as *hoi polloi*), try another word.

holistic

If you mean considering a person or subject as a whole (as in a *holistic admissions process* at a university that considers more than academic results), *holistic* is just about acceptable. But if tempted to use it in other contexts, take a holistic approach to the English lexicon and see if something else will work. If you merely mean *wide-ranging*, say that.

home

When you read "*she had seven homes in four continents*," you inevitably wonder whether any of them was truly a home, not just a *house*. As a generic term, *home* can be usefully vague if some of them were flats or chalets. If possible, though, be precise and write *house* or *shack* or *castle*: home is where the heart is.

home in

This phrase does not involve sharpening a knife, so it is not *hone in on*. You *home in on* something, like a homing pigeon does.

homogeneous, homogenous

Homogeneous means *of the same kind or nature*, has five syllables and a second e, and is almost certainly the word you want. (*Homogenous* means similar because of common descent, and is a near synonym of *homogenetic* or *homologous*.)

homosexual

Homosexual comes from the Greek word *homos* (same), not the Latin word *homo* (man). So it applies as much to women as to men. But use it to refer to acts or attractions, not people, who may or may not consider themselves **gay** (qv).

hopefully

Many authorities agree that it is outmoded to object to the use of *hopefully* to mean *it is hoped that*. In *The Economist*, however, we may well begin an article hopefully, but (even though it is not grammatically wrong) we do not write *Hopefully, it will be finished by Wednesday*. Try *With luck, if all goes well, it is hoped that...*

hypothermia, hyperthermia

Hypothermia is what kills old folk in winter. If you say it is *hyperthermia*, that means they have been *carried off by heat stroke*.

immanent, imminent

Immanent means *pervading* or *inherent*, and originates in theology. You probably want *imminent*, which means *threatening* or *impending*. An immanent God is not necessarily about to make a second coming.

immolate

Immolate means to *sacrifice*, usually but not necessarily by burning, though this is what any reader will understand by *self-immolation*.

important

If something is *important*, say why and to whom. Use sparingly, and avoid such unexplained claims as *this important house, the most important painter of the 20th century.*

impracticable, impractical

If something is *impracticable*, it *cannot be done*. If it's *impractical*, it is *not worth trying to do it*. See also **practicable, practical.**

inchoate

Inchoate means *not yet fully developed*. It is not the same as *incoherent* or (despite the deceptively similar spelling) *chaotic*.

indicted

Be careful. Someone you are tempted to call an *indicted war criminal* may be acquitted, and in that case, legally no war criminal at all—a fact that his libel lawyers may soon remind us of. Prefer *indicted for war crimes*.

individual

Used occasionally, the noun *individual* can be a useful colloquial term for *chap* or *bloke* or *guy*. "*In a corner, Parker, a grave, lean individual, bent over the chafing-dish, in which he was preparing for his employer and his guest their simple lunch*" (P.G. Wodehouse).

Used indiscriminately for *person* or, in the plural, *people*, it becomes bureaucratic. "*Individuals desiring to function as operators using instruments listed under paragraph (A)(3) of rule 3701-53-02 of the Administrative Code shall apply to the director of health for permits on forms prescribed and provided by the director of health*" (Ohio Department of Health).

initial, initially

Prefer *first, at first.*

interesting

Like **important** (qv) and *funny*, *interesting* makes assumptions that may not be shared by the reader. Facts and stories introduced as interesting often turn out to be something else: *Interestingly, my father-in-law was born in Dorking.* If something really is interesting, you probably do not need to say so.

investigations

Investigations *of*, not *into*.

ironically

Purists like to say that *ironically* is often used nowadays in a way that has little to do with irony. Ironically, they are often wrong. *Irony*, from the Greek word for *dissimulation*, originally meant the Socratic method of discussion by feigning ignorance. Then it came to mean *a figure of speech, used sarcastically or satirically, in which the intended meaning is the opposite of the literal meaning.* And with that came the meaning of *a contradictory outcome of events involving mockery by fate or fortune.* This is how it is often used today. Nothing wrong with that. But it should not be used to mean merely *surprisingly* or *coincidentally*.

Islam, Islamism, jihadist, mujahideen

Islamic means relating to *Islam*; it is a synonym of the adjective Muslim and is best used in the context of religion. Use *Islamist* rather than *Islamic* when referring to a political ideology that purports to be based on *Islam*. Do not refer to Iran as the *Islamic Republic*. *Afghanistan*, *Mauritania* and *Pakistan* are also Islamic republics; many other countries make reference to Islam in their constitutions.

Islamism encompasses a wide range of views—from the constitutionalist Justice and Development Party in power in Morocco, to Egypt's ousted Muslim Brotherhood, the Hamas movement in Gaza, al-Qaeda and the gore-loving Islamic State. At the moderate end of the spectrum you can talk of *political* or *moderate Islamists*. (Members of Tunisia's Ennahda now want to call themselves *Muslim democrats*.) At the more extreme end you can talk of *radical*, *militant* or even *violent*

Islamists. For those who exalt violent jihad as a core belief, eg, al-Qaeda, call them *jihadists* (see details below).

Avoid referring to *Islamic State* with the definite article. Its ideology is an outlier in the world of Islam. You may, if you want, qualify its title in some way, eg, *the jihadists of Islamic State* or *the Islamic State group*. Similarly, qualify the short-lived entity it created in Iraq and Syria in 2014 as a *"caliphate"* (inverted commas needed) or *would-be caliphate*.

Jihad is the Arabic word for *striving*. For modern Muslims, it may mean *military war to propagate Islamism*, ie, to spread Islam as a religious, political and social ideology (*jihad* of the sword). Or it may mean *spiritual struggle* for personal purification and moral betterment (*jihad* against oneself). Or it may merely mean *doing right*, improving society and being virtuous (*jihad* of the tongue or of the hand). A religious obligation for all Muslims, *jihad* is for most a non-violent duty. Do not therefore use it simply to mean *holy war*. Rather make clear what sort of *jihad* is under discussion in the context.

Someone engaged in *jihad* is a *mujahid* (plural, *mujahideen*) or a *jihadist* (prefer to *jihadi*). In practice, these terms nowadays are always used of Muslims engaged in an *armed struggle*, though *mujahideen* may simply be Muslim *militants fighting for a cause* whereas *jihadists* are always *fighting to spread Islamism by force*.

issues

The Economist has *issues*—one each week—but if you think you have *issues* with *The Economist*, you probably mean you have *complaints*, *irritations* or *delivery difficulties*. If you *disagree* with *The Economist*, you may *take issue* with it. Do not use *issue* as a synonym for *problem*.

jejune

Jejune means *insipid*, *unsatisfying*, *lacking in substance*. It comes from the Latin *jejunus*, meaning *fasting*, *barren* or *unproductive*, and has nothing to do with the French word *jeune*, meaning *young*.

jib, gibe, gybe

Jib (noun): *sail* or *boom of a crane*

Jib (verb): to *balk* or *shy*
Gibe (noun): *taunt*
Gibe (verb): to *scoff* or *flout*
Gybe (verb): to *alter course*.

Don't *jibe*.

judgment call

Prefer *judgment* or *matter of judgment*.

key

This overused word is a noun and, like most nouns, may modify another (as in *the key ministries*). Do not, however, use it as a free-standing adjective, as in *The choice of running-mate is key*.

lag

If you *lag* transitively, you may be insulating a pipe or a loft. But anything failing to keep up with a front-runner, rate of growth, fourth-quarter profit or whatever is *lagging behind* it.

lama, llama

Lama: priest. *Llama*: beast.

last

For *most recent*, as in *the last issue of The Economist*, prefer *last week's* or *the latest issue* instead. *Last year*, in 2023, means 2022; if you mean the 12 months up to the time of writing, write *the past year*. The same goes for *the past month*, *past week*, *past* (not last) *ten years*.

Last week is best avoided; anyone reading those words several days after publication may be confused. Prefer a date, or *recently*.

To an MP who asked if he had heard his last speech, John Philpot Curran (1750-1817) responded, "I hope I have."

Latin names

When it is necessary to use a Latin name for animals, plants, etc, follow the standard practice. Thus for all creatures higher than viruses, write the binomial name in italics, giving an initial capital to the first word (the genus): *Turdus turdus*, the songthrush; *Squamocnus brevidentis*, the strawberry sea cucumber. This rule also applies to *Homo sapiens* and to such uses as *Homo economicus*. On second mention, the genus may be abbreviated (*T. turdus*). In some species, such as dinosaurs, the genus alone is used in lieu of a common name: *Diplodocus*, *Tyrannosaurus*. Also *Drosophila*, a fruit fly favoured by geneticists. But *Escherichia coli*, a bacterium also favoured by geneticists, is known universally as *E. coli*, even on first mention.

Latin phrases

It is generally best (and usually easy) to translate them. Use not *per capita* but *per person*. And not *per annum* but *per year*, *each year* or *annually*.

lay, lie

To lay is transitive, meaning to place something down: a *carpet*, a *trap*, a *bet* or a *bunch of keys*. But *lay* is also the past tense of the verb to *lie*: "As I Lay Dying". You may *lay your head upon someone's shoulder* and she may be *lying down*, but if you say *She was laying there* it suggests she was about to produce an egg.

to place something: *I lay, I laid, I have laid*
to recline: *I lie, I lay, I have lain*
to tell an untruth: *I lie, I lied, I have lied*

legacy

It is now common to use *legacy*, which once meant *a bequest of personal property*, to modify anything that outlives the thing with which it was originally associated. So dead musicians live on through *legacy bands* and the Olympic games have *legacy obligations*. If you use *legacy* in one of these senses, make sure the meaning is clear, or find another word.

leverage

If you cannot find a way of avoiding the word *leverage*, explain what it means. In its technical financial sense, as a noun, it may mean *the ratio of long-term debt to total capital employed*. But note that *operating leverage* and *financial leverage* are different.

LGBT+

When referring to advocates of rights for lesbians, gay men, bisexuals, transgender people and other identities, you can use *LGBT+* as an umbrella term. Avoid reference to the *LGBT+ community* (or any other **community**, qv), because activists for one particular issue do not represent all people. Because LGBT + is a broad term, usually it is most accurate to refer to a specific group of people.

like, unlike

Like governs nouns and pronouns. Many people use it to govern prepositions and verbs too, as in *like in America, like I was saying*. But in writing, *as* is better: *as in America, as I was saying*. *Like* has a convenient antonym, *unlike*, which in informal use allows phrases like *unlike when I was a child*. There is no negative counterpart for *as*, so you have to do a radical restructuring of the sentence to express the same thoughts in print.

To help you remember old-fashioned *as*:

Like the hart panteth for the water brooks I pant for a revival of Shakespeare's "Like You Like It".
I can see tense draftees relax and purr
When the sergeant barks, "Like you were."
–And don't try to tell me that our well has been defiled by immigration;
Like goes Madison Avenue, like so goes the nation.

(Ogden Nash)

If you find yourself writing *She looked like she had had enough* or *It seemed like he was running out of puff*, you should replace *like* with *as if* or *as though*.

But *authorities like Fowler and Gowers* is a perfectly acceptable alternative to *authorities such as Fowler and Gowers*, if what you mean is *authorities who are like Fowler and Gowers. Such as* introduces examples, *like* introduces resemblances, and the two overlap.

likely

Likely is still predominantly an adjective in British English. Avoid adverbial constructions such as *He will likely announce the date on Monday* and *The price will likely fall when results are posted Friday.* Use *He is likely to announce...* or *The price will probably fall...*

literally

Many predecessors of *literally* (like *really, truly* and *very*) began life as meaning "in truth or reality" (per the Oxford English Dictionary on *very*), but are now mere intensifiers. *Literally* is still holding its ground meaning "not figuratively", and is the only word doing that job. Do not write *it was literally raining cats and dogs* unless something very strange has happened.

loaded words

Certain words, in certain contexts come with assumptions that may not be universal: **affordable** (qv), **important** (qv), *(in)appropriate*, **interesting** (qv), *matters* (as in *"This matters"*), *relevant*, **sustainable** (qv). If it is interesting or relevant, say why and to whom.

locate

Locate, in any of its forms, can usually be replaced. *The missing scientist was located* means he was *found. The diplomats will meet at a secret location* means either that they will meet *in a secret place* or meet *secretly. A company located in Texas* is simply *a company in Texas.*

logistics

The science of distribution of goods by road, rail and air.

luxurious, luxuriant

Luxurious means *indulgently pleasurable*. *Luxuriant* means *exuberant* or *profuse*. Someone on the street with a *luxuriant beard* may not lead a *luxurious life*.

majority

A rule for *majority* and verb agreement: When used in an abstract sense, it takes the singular; when it is used to denote the elements making up the majority, it should be plural. *A two-thirds majority is needed to amend the constitution*, but *A majority of the Senate were opposed*.

media

Prefer *press* if the context allows it. If you have to use *media*, remember they are plural.

mendacious, mendicant

Mendacious means *lying*. *Mendicant* means a *beggar* or *begging*.

meta-

The prefix *meta-*, from the Greek word for *with*, *beyond* or *after*, has long been used before the name of a science to designate what the Oxford English Dictionary calls a higher science of the same nature but dealing with ulterior problems (eg, metachemistry, metaphysiology). This, says the OED, is done in supposed analogy to metaphysics (which is misapprehended as meaning the science of that which transcends the physical).

Philosophers have extended the usage to, eg, *metalanguage* (ie, language about language), *metatheorems* and indeed to anything that is consciously self-referential. Computer geeks have fallen on it with delight, coining *meta-elements*, *metadata*, *metatags* and the name for Facebook's parent company. But do not follow the trend of adding *meta-* to anything to lend it gravitas.

mete, meet

You may *mete out punishment*, but if it is to fit the crime that punishment is *meet*.

meter, metre, metrics

A *meter* is a gadget for measuring. A *metre* is a unit of length. *Metrics* is the theory of measurement or the study of metrical structures in verse. Do not use the term as a pretentious word for *figures*, *numbers* or *measurements* themselves, as in "I can't take the metrics I'm privileged to and work my way to a number in [that] range." (General Thomas Metz, talking about the number of insurgents killed in Iraq.)

migrate

Birds, animals and people *migrate*, intransitively, from place to place. If talking about copying computer files or bureaucrats relocating their offices, transitively *move* them.

military

Try to avoid *military* as a noun, writing *the army* or another service instead. (And definitely avoid the Americanism *served in the military*, which can always be replaced with a specific service if you are talking about a single person.) But the integration of modern forces makes the overarching noun *the military* all but inevitable in certain contexts. Use judiciously, seeing if you can replace with *armed forces*.

mitigate, militate

Mitigates *mollifies*, *tempers* or *helps to excuse*; militates *tells (against)*.

momentarily

Use it to mean *for a moment*. If you want *in a moment*, use *soon*.

monopoly, monopsony

A *monopolist* is a sole seller; a sole buyer is a *monopsonist*.

moot

Moot, in British English, means *arguable*, *doubtful* or *open to debate*. Americans use it to mean *hypothetical*, ie, *of no practical significance*. If you use the word, use it in the British sense, making sure the meaning is clear in context. But it is usually best reworded.

mortar

If not a vessel in which herbs, etc, are pounded with a pestle, a *mortar* is a piece of artillery for throwing a shell, bomb or lifeline. Do not write *He was hit by a mortar* unless he was improbably struck by the artillery piece. It is *hit by a mortar shell*.

move

Do not use the noun *move* if you mean *decision*, *bid*, *deal*, *action* or something more precise. But use the verb *move* rather than *relocate*.

multiple

Do you mean *a number of* or *several* or *many* when you write *there were multiple offers*? If so, use one of those.

named after

Named after, not *for*.

nauseate, nauseous

Nauseous nauseates style-book writers. It has meant both *causing nausea* and *prone to experiencing nausea* since the early 17th century. But today the overwhelming majority use it to mean *feeling nausea*. Write *nauseating* for sick-making. Use either *nauseous* or (if there is any risk of ambiguity) *nauseated* for *feeling sick*.

noisome

Noisome means *noxious*, *harmful* or *offensive* to the eyes or nose—but not the ears: that is *noisy*.

none, neither, nor

Try to use *none* with a singular verb, especially when the sense indicates that each item is to be considered individually: *None of these options was acceptable*. But when a group is considered as a group, the plural is acceptable: *None of his friends are coming*. When modified, *none* needs the plural too: *Almost none of her ministers were willing to stand up to her*.

Neither a nor b (or *either*) does take singular agreement, unless b is plural. So *Neither the Frenchman nor the German has done it*, but *Neither the Dutchman nor the Danes have done it*, where the verb agrees with the element closest to it.

Nor should not be preceded by *and*. You may, however, start a sentence with it.

number (singular or plural)

Regarding singular or plural verb agreement, remember:

The number is (staggering, unimpressive)..., where *number* is synonymous with a *figure*.

But *A number are* (opposed, upset).

one

Try to avoid *one* as a personal pronoun. *You* will often do instead.

only

Put *only* as close as you can to the words it qualifies, to avoid ambiguity:

They discussed Taiwan only briefly (not at length)
They discussed only Taiwan briefly (and other topics at length)
They only discussed Taiwan briefly (and did nothing else)
Only they discussed Taiwan briefly (and no one else)

onto

On and *to* should be run together when they are closely linked, as in *He pranced onto the stage*. If, however, the sense of the sentence makes the *on* closer to the preceding word, or the *to* closer to the succeeding word, than they are to each other, keep them separate: *He pranced on to the next town* or *He pranced on to wild applause.*

ophthalmology, optometry, optics

Ophthalmology is the branch of medicine concerning the health of the eyes. *Optometry* is the measurement of their refractive power, or of lenses, as when you get glasses. *Optics* is the science of light.

Do not use *optics* to glamorise mere *impressions* or *appearances*, as in *The optics of wearing a designer dress to a disaster site could be unfortunate.*

overseas

Overseas should not be used to mean merely *abroad* or *foreign.*

oxymoron

An *oxymoron* is traditionally deliberate, for rhetorical effect: *bitter-sweet, cruel kindness, friendly fire, open secret, sweet sorrow*, etc. For the unintentionally contrasting juxtaposition, try *contradiction in terms.*

palate, pallet, palette

Your *palate* is the roof of your mouth (or your capacity to appreciate food and drink). A *pallet* is a mattress on which you may sleep or a wooden frame for use with fork-lift trucks. Mix paints on a *palette.*

parse

Parse, meaning to *describe a word's part of speech, case, number, gender* and so on, or to *describe the structural relationships of a sentence*, is often now used in journalese (see pp. 27-9) to mean *analyse*. Unless you really mean close linguistic analysis, choose a plainer word.

peer

A *peer* is not a contemporary, colleague or counterpart but an *equal.*

picaresque, picturesque

Picaresque means *roguish* or *knavish*, often in adventures and originally in the context of fiction. *Picturesque* means pretty as (in) a picture.

populace

This term means the *common people* (**hoi polloi**, qv) to many. Use *population* if you mean everyone.

positive

Do not over-use where other words will do. *A positive meeting* is possibly a *fruitful* one. *Positive results* might be *encouraging* ones, unless in a medical context where a *positive diagnosis* is bad.

possessives

It is fine to say *a friend of Dave's*, just as you would say *a friend of mine*, so you can also say *a friend of Dave's and Sam's*. It is also fine to say *a friend of Dave*, or *a friend of Dave and Sam*. What you must not say is *Dave and Sam's friend*. If you wish to use that construction, you must say *Dave's and Sam's friend*, which is cumbersome. But *Sam & Dave* were a musical duo; considering them as an act under that name, you can refer to *Sam & Dave's records*. (See The "false possessive", pp. 52-3.)

possessives (comparing)

Take care to compare possessives with possessives: *The Belgian economy is bigger than Russia* should be *Belgium's economy is bigger than Russia's*. An advertisement for *The Economist* declared that *Our style and our whole philosophy are different from other publications*. That should be *publications'*, or *different from that of other publications*.

power, energy

Power refers to the rate at which energy is transferred. It is most often measured in *watts* (and *megawatts*, *gigawatts*, etc). A solar farm or nuclear reactor will be rated for its power to light streets and heat homes at any given time.

Energy measures power applied over time, and so in these

contexts is measured in *watt-hours, megawatt-hours*, etc (see also Abbreviations, pp. 147-9). These are the amount of energy used when a watt or megawatt is applied for an hour.

practicable, practical

Practicable means *feasible. Practical* means *useful* or *handy*. See also **impracticable, impractical**.

pre-

Pre- is often unnecessary, as in *pre-announce, precondition, pre-board, pre-ordered, pre-packaged, pre-prepared, pre-cooked*. If it seems to be doing something useful, try making use of a word such as *already* or *earlier*: *Here's one I cooked earlier.*

   Pre-owned is *second-hand*. See also **reshuffle, resupply**, and Redundancy on pp. 33-4.

precipitate, precipitous

Precipitate (adj) means *rash, hasty* or *headlong. Precipitous* means *sheer* or like a *precipice*. It is therefore unlikely that *trade fell precipitately*, as *The Economist* reported (July 25th 2009).

presently

Presently means *soon* in Britain and *now* in America. So use *soon* or *now* instead.

press, pressure, pressurise

Pressurise is what you want in an aircraft, but not in an argument or encounter where persuasion is being employed. The verb you want there is *press* (use *pressure* only as a noun).

prevaricate, procrastinate

Prevaricate means *evade the truth; procrastinate* means *delay*. "Procrastination"—or punctuality, if you are Oscar Wilde—"is the thief of time."

process

Process is usually unnecessary. Some writers see their prose in industrial terms: *education* becomes an *education process*, *consultation* a consultation process, *elections* an *electoral process*, *development* a *development process*, *writing* a *writing process*. That said, *peace process* is allowed, as it is often quite different from actual peace.

prodigal

If you are *prodigal*, that does not mean you are *welcomed home, forgiven* or taken back without recrimination. The Bible's prodigal son was so called because he was *wasteful* and *reckless* first.

profession

By convention, *professions* are those like law, medicine and accounting, which require of their members some degree of learning, usually tested in an examination, and are regulated by a responsible body. Journalists and bankers, though they may be *professional* in the sense that, unlike amateurs, they do what they do for money, are therefore not members of a profession. Try *trade*.

propaganda

Propaganda (which is singular) means *a systematic effort to spread doctrine or opinions*. It is not a synonym for *lies*.

protagonist

Protagonist means the *chief actor or combatant*. If you are referring to several people in a single encounter or endeavour, only one can be a *protagonist*.

pry

Use *prise*, unless you mean *peer* or *peep*.

raise, raze

To *raise* means to *lift*. To *raze* means pretty much the opposite: to *lay level* (with the ground) or *erase*. No need to say *razed to the ground*.

rebut, refute

Rebut means *meet in argument*. *Refute* is stronger. It means *disprove*. Neither should be used as a synonym for *deny*.

red and blue

See **blue and red**.

redact

Redact is used to mean *obscure, blot out, obliterate*. Use it only in this legal/technical sense.

redolent

Redolent means *smelling of, fragrant*. Do not therefore write *redolent of the smell of linseed oil*.

reduce, diminish, lessen, shrink

These words are not interchangeable. *Reduce* is transitive, so must be followed by a noun. *Diminish* and *shrink* can be transitive or intransitive. So can *lessen*, though it is usually used transitively.

regime, regimen

A *regime* is a system of government. Use *regimen* for a course of diet and exercise.

relationship

Relationship is a long word often better replaced by *relations*. *The two countries hope for a better relationship* means *The two countries hope for better relations*.

relatively

Keep this for when you really mean in relation to something else: *If you are used to London, Berlin is relatively inexpensive.* If you just mean *fairly, somewhat,* say that.

report

Report on, not *into.*

reshuffle, resupply

Shuffle and *supply* will do.

revert

Revert means *return to* or *go back to,* as in *The garden has reverted to wilderness.* It does not mean *come back to* or *get back to,* as in *I'll give you an answer as soon as I can.*

rock

In Britain a *rock* is too large to throw; protesters use *stones.*

same

Often superfluous. If your sentence contains *on the same day that,* try *on the day that.*

sanction

Do not use *sanction* as a verb to mean to *impose sanctions on,* because it traditionally means the reverse, to *approve* or *bless.* If you want a verb, try *penalise, punish,* etc.

scale, scalable

It is growing hard to avoid the jargony verb *to scale* and its adjective *scalable* to describe innovations, growing companies, development solutions and the like. But alternatives exist and may be clearer: try to say if something can be *rolled out quickly, grown sustainably, produced in large quantities cheaply,* etc.

scotch, Scotch, Scottish, Scots

To *scotch* means to *slash* or *disable*, not to destroy. ("We have scotch'd the snake, not killed it," Macbeth).

The adjective *Scotch* may describe products like *whisky*, *beef* or *eggs*. But the people are *Scottish* (adj) or *Scots* (n). *Scots* is also the name of the dialect of the region, made famous by Robert Burns (which is not just *Scottish English*). The Celtic language is called *(Scottish) Gaelic*.

The term *scot-free* means free from punishment (originally a fine), not free from Scots.

second-biggest, etc

Second-biggest (*third-oldest*, etc): think before you write. *Apart from New York, a Bramley is the second-biggest apple in the world. Other than home-making and parenting, prostitution is the third-oldest profession.* These should be *Apart from New York, a Bramley is the biggest apple in the world*, etc.

secret, secretive

Places, meetings or documents can be *secret*, but only people or their methods can be *secretive*.

sensual, sensuous

Sensual means *carnal* or *voluptuous*. *Sensuous* means pertaining to aesthetic appreciation, without any implication of lasciviousness.

sequestered, sequestrated

Sequestered means *secluded*. *Sequestrated* means *confiscated* or *made bankrupt*.

shrug

This means *to draw up the shoulders*, so do not write *She shrugged her shoulders*. (See Redundancy, pp. 33-4.)

silicon, silicone

Silicon is a common element used as a semiconductor to make electronic circuits smaller. *Silicone* is a compound of silicon best known for its use in rubbery tools and artificial body parts.

simplistic

Prefer *simple-minded, naive*.

singular or plural?

Propaganda looks plural but is not. *Billiards, bowls, darts* and *fives* are also singular. *Law and order*, like *hue and cry* and a *ham and cheese*, are really singular concepts and take singular verbs.

Meanwhile *media* are plural. So are *whereabouts* and *headquarters*. Teams that take the name of a town, country or university are plural, even when they look singular: *England were bowled out for 56*.

See also **data**, which can be both singular and plural.

Prefer the singular when referring to *chemical* (not *chemicals*) *companies, drug* (not *drugs*) *traffickers, pension* (not *pensions*) *systems* and so on. But *arms-trader, drinks group, groundsman* and *sales force*.

Do not assume that all voting is done in *elections* in the plural. If, as in the United States, several votes (for the presidency, the Senate, the House of Representatives, etc) are held on the same day, it is correct to talk about *elections*. The European Parliament's elections should also be plural. But in, say, Britain parliamentary polls are usually held on their own, in a single *general election*.

The opposition demanded an election is often preferable to *The opposition demanded fresh elections*. And to write *The next presidential elections are due in 2025* suggests there will be more than one presidential poll in that year.

skyrocketed

Rocketed is graphic enough. Avoid *skyrocketing*.

slither, sliver

As a noun, *slither* is *scree*. As a verb, it means *slide*. If you mean a *slice*, the word you want is *sliver*.

smart

In British English, *smart* means *well dressed*, but *smart sanctions*, *smart weapons*, *smartphones* and all else of that nature are now with us for good. In fact, the word is now so over-used that if you merely mean *clever* or *elegant* (of people), say so.

socialise

The original British meaning of *socialise* was to make someone ready for society, a usage appropriated by social scientists to discuss how (for example) children are taught their social roles, for good or ill. Americans, meanwhile, use *socialise* to mean *getting together for a drink*.

soft-spoken

If you have a quiet voice you are *soft*—not *softly*—*spoken*.

soi-disant

Soi-disant means *self-styled*, not *so-called*.

specific

Do not use in the singular to mean a *detail*; a *specific* is a *medicine* or *remedy*. But in the plural *specifics* are allowed.

stanch, staunch

Stanch the flow, though the man be *staunch* (*stout*). The words are quite distinct in English, but share a common root.

stentorian, stertorous

Stentorian means *loud* (like the voice of Stentor, a warrior in the Trojan war). *Stertorous* means *characterised by a snoring sound* (from the Latin *stertere*, to snore).

straight, strait

Straight means *direct* or *uncurved*; *strait* means *narrow* or *tight*. The *straight and narrow* is so written because *strait and narrow* would be redundant. The *strait-laced* tend to be *straight-faced*.

strategy

Strategy, in military contexts, is distinguished from **tactics** (qv). You fight battles with tactics, and win the war with a strategy. But in other contexts, especially business, *strategy* is much overused to dignify a mere *plan*.

-style

Avoid *German-style supervisory boards*, an EU-*style rotating presidency*, etc. Explain what you mean.

subcontract

If you engage someone to do something, you are *contracting* the job; only if the contractor then asks someone else to do it is the job *subcontracted*.

sustainable

A *sustainable business* is one that will not go bust. A *sustainable-energy business* is trying to make energy from algae, etc. *Sustainable farming* is trying not to exhaust the land in the process.

swath, swathe

A *swath* was originally the *area covered by the reaper's scythe*, and by extension a *broad sweep of land*. A *swathe* was a *band of linen* in which, for instance, a child may be wrapped. *Swathe* has so long been an alternative spelling of *swath* that many people pronounce the two in the same way (rhyming with *bathe*). The distinction between them is all but lost, so use *swathe* for both.

systemic, systematic

Systemic means *relating to a system or body as a whole*. *Systematic* means *according to system*, or *methodical*.

table

Avoid *table* as a transitive verb. In Britain *to table* means to *bring something forward for action*. In America it means the opposite, ie, *to shelve*.

tactics

Whether in battle or in politics, use for *day-to-day techniques* as opposed to **strategy** (qv), the long-term plan.

terrorist

Use these words with care. Prefer *terrorism* to *terror* when you refer to the use of violence by non-state actors in an organised system of intimidation for political ends. A *terrorist* is someone who resorts to such methods. Prefer *suspected terrorists* to *terrorist suspects*.

Not every act of revolting violence is terrorism. Terrorism is not aimed at its direct victims only. It is intended to spread fear widely, to advance political ends (even those that may seem incoherent). Modifiers can help you specify: *jihadist terrorism, white-supremacist terrorism*.

State-sponsored terror (not *terrorism*) is an acceptable term for violence intended to shock and cow a population. *The Terror* during the French revolution is a clear example.

testament, testimony

A *testament* is a *will*, and *testimony* is *evidence*. It is *testimony* to the trickiness of these similar words that *testament* often appears in its place.

the

The, known as the definite article, is to be used with discrimination. The Oxford English Dictionary gives it 23 definitions, with dozens of sub-entries. *The Economist*'s use carries some particularities.

We refer to Barclays as *a* British bank, not *the* British bank, because there are other British banks, and one of the uses of *the* is to define. You should not, on first mention, refer to *the son of the king* if the king has more than one son.

But *the* is also used for things already mentioned, or so well known that it can be assumed the reader knows them. So *Ford, a car company* might seem otherworldly when most people expect *Ford, the car company*. In cases like this, you can, on first mention, add a descriptor: *Ford, America's second-biggest car company*. Or if your subject is indeed likely to be known to readers, skip the identifier on first mention, and use a synonym on second mention. *Ford announced that it would open a new plant in Spain. America's second-biggest car company wants to expand its electric-car business in Europe...*

Occasionally, the definite article may be optional: *Maximilien Robespierre, the leader of the Committee of Public Safety*, is preferable to *Maximilien Robespierre, leader of the Committee of Public Safety*, but in this context the *the* after *Robespierre* is not essential. However, *Leaders of both mainstream parties* means something different from *The leaders of both mainstream parties*.

throe, throw

Throes are *spasms* or *pangs. Throw* is *the act of casting or hurling through the air. Last throws* are all right on the cricket pitch, but *last throes* are more likely on the battlefield (or in metaphorical extensions evoking death spasms).

times (x)

Be careful. Avoid *three times more than (higher than) x*. It traditionally means *four times as much as x* (three times added onto the original number) but too many readers take it to mean *three times as much as x*. Instead, write *gas prices are nine times what they were at this time last year*. (See Chapter 4 for discussion of base rates and sensible comparisons.)

tortuous, torturous

Tortuous means *winding* or *twisting*. *Torturous* means *causing torture*.

tragedy, travesty

A *travesty* is (originally) a *disguise* or (today) an *absurdly inadequate representation of someone or something*, as in *a travesty of justice*.

A tragedy is a *dramatically sad event*.

transgender

On first mention, when appropriate, describe someone who has transitioned to being a man as a *transgender man* and one who has transitioned to being a woman a *transgender woman*. On second mention, it is *trans man* and *trans woman* with a space.

transitive and intransitive verbs

Some verbs are intransitive (with no direct object, as in *She slept*) and others are transitive (taking a direct object, as in *He saw her*). Some can be both (as in *They ate* or *They ate dinner*).

Some transitive verbs drift towards intransitive use, which can be faddish. Avoid the usages on the left in favour of those on the right:

He committed to doing better	*He committed himself to doing better*
The stocks depleted by half	*The stocks were depleted by half*
He delivers	*He delivers what he promises*
Bonuses reduced this year	*The board reduced bonuses this year*
The growth rate halved	*The growth rate fell by half*

On the other hand, some verbs should not be used transitively. They should either take a preposition or be replaced with another verb.

They agreed a new deal	*They agreed on a new deal*
The snow collapsed the roof	*The roof collapsed under the snow*
We want to grow the business	*We want to make the business grow*
Students are protesting the cuts	*Students are protesting against the cuts*

He appealed the ruling	*He appealed against the ruling*
The speaker progressed the bill	*The speaker advanced the bill*
Wage growth has lagged inflation	*Wage growth has lagged behind inflation*
Reserves totalled 10bn barrels	*Reserves amounted to 10bn barrels*
The passengers disembarked the plane	*The crew disembarked the passengers*
The government targeted aid at the poor	*The government directed aid to the poor*

transpire

Transpire originally meant (for vapour) to pass through the walls of a surface, or (for an animal) to exhale. It then meant *"to pass from secrecy into light"* (Samuel Johnson) and then came to be a pretentious synonym for *to happen*. Unless you mean the physical sense, use *come to light* or *happen*.

troika

Troika, a word for a *Russian vehicle drawn by three horses abreast*, is now inexplicably fashionable. Use it when it is unavoidable (as in the much-mentioned troika of the IMF, European Central Bank and European Commission during the euro-zone crisis). But avoid proliferation of this word when *trio* or *threesome* will do as well.

trooper, trouper

A *trooper* is a *cavalry soldier*. Some other non-cavalry units employ the rank of trooper as well.

But if prefixed by *old*, what you want is *trouper*, an old *member of a theatrical company*, or perhaps a *good sort*.

try to, try and

Try to choose *try to* over the chatty *try and*.

twinkle, twinkling

In the twinkling of an eye means *in a very short time*.

Before he was even a twinkle in his father's eye means *Before (perhaps just before) he was conceived*. So, more loosely, *Before the Model T was even a twinkle in Henry Ford's eye* could mean *Before Henry Ford was even thinking about a mass-produced car.*

use and abuse

Use and abuse: much used and abused. People *take* drugs, not *use* them. And *drug abuse* is just *drug taking*, unless it is misuse of prescription drugs.

venal, venial

Venal means *unprincipled, capable of being bribed, subject to corrupt influences*, etc.

Venial is a forgivable class of sins in Christianity, ranked below the *mortal sins*. To swap these often-confused words may be a *venial sin*, but do not commit it anyway.

venerable

Venerable means *worthy of reverence*. Do not use to mean merely old.

verbal, oral

Every agreement, except those of the nod-and-wink variety, is *verbal*. If you mean one that was not written down, describe it as *oral*.

via

The Latin *via* means *by way of*. So too in English. Use it therefore to say *He flew to hell via Atlanta, but he booked his journey through* [not *via*] *an ecclesiastical travel agent, whom he reached by driving along* [not *via*] *a road paved with good intentions.*

-ward, -wards

When it forms part of an adjective, the suffix *-ward* should not take an *s*: a *backward somersault*, an *eastward glance*. As part of an adverb, either *-ward* or *-wards* may be correct. But where there are alternatives,

-wards is often preferred in British English: *he went backwards, towards the house* or *onwards and upwards*.

while

Not *whilst*.

wiggle, wriggle

By all means *wiggle your hips*, but if you need space in which to do it, or something else, that is *wriggle room*.

words ending both -ed and -t

Burned or *burnt? Dreamed* or *dreamt? Dwelled* or *dwelt? Leaped* or *leapt? Learned* or *learnt? Smelled* or *smelt? Spelled* or *spelt? Spilled* or *spilt? Spoiled* or *spoilt?* Modern British English allows both. Some attribute a greater passage of time to versions of the past tense or participle that end *-ed*: *And therefore when her aunt returned, Matilda and the house were burned* perhaps implies a slower event than *He burnt his fingers*. But no such distinction can be made where *learning* and *spelling* are concerned. In time the *-ed* versions may disappear, as *meaned* has since the 19th century. At present, though, neither version is wrong.

The same goes for these other competing past tenses and participles: *bereaved, bereft; beseeched, besought; cleaved, cleft; kneeled, knelt*. But use *pleaded*, not *pled*, both in legal contexts and in those like *He pleaded for his life*. See Chapter 9 on Americanisms.

words ending -ee

Absentees, bargees, bootees, employees, evacuees, detainees, devotees, divorcees (male or female), *jamborees, levees, licensees, payees, referees, refugees* and *trustees* are fine.

But please no *attendees* (those attending), *draftees* (conscripts), *enrollees* (participants), *escapees* (escapers), *indictees* (the indicted), *mentees* (the mentored), *retirees* (the retired), *returnees* (people sent back or going home), *standees* (standing passengers) or *tutees* (the tutored).

worth

When the word *worth* follows a sum, measurement or quantity, an apostrophe is needed: *three months' worth of exports, a lifetime's worth of dashed hopes.* Note: *$25m-worth* is an exception.

wrack, rack, wreak, wrought

Wrack is an old noun meaning *vengeance, punishment* or *wreckage* (as in *wrack and ruin*). As a verb it can mean to *devastate*.

It has nothing to do with a *rack*, as in a frame on which you might put toast. Such a frame was once used to torture people by stretching them. So if you mean something like torture, you want *racked* (*with pain, guilt*, etc). *Rack* your brains, ie, stretch them until they give up what you need. You do not want to *wrack* them—that would be devastating.

Since wars, drought, etc, both torture and devastate, both *racked by war* and *wracked by war* are acceptable, depending on the sense you intend.

To *wreak* is to *bring about* or *inflict*, as in *damage, destruction* or *havoc.* Its past tense and past participle is *wreaked.* (It is not *wrought*, an alternative past tense of *work*, as in *wrought iron*, or iron that has been worked.)

7

Sweating the small stuff: punctuation and mechanics

This chapter includes information on all of the small but critical things needed to put together a readable, consistent piece of prose, including many universal rules as well as some that are distinctive elements of *The Economist*'s house style.

Punctuation

apostrophes

Use the normal possessive ending 's after singular words or names that end in s: *boss's, caucus's, Delors's, St James's*. Use it, too, after plurals that do not end in s: *children's, Frenchmen's, media's*.

Use the ending s' on plurals that end in s—*Danes', bosses', Joneses'*—including plural names that take a singular verb, eg, *Reuters', Barclays'*.

Although singular in other respects, *the United States, the United Nations, the Philippines*, etc, have a plural possessive apostrophe: eg, *Who will be the United States' next president?*

People's = of (the) people. *Peoples'* = of peoples.

Try to avoid using *Lloyd's* (the insurance market) as a possessive; like *Christie's* and *Sotheby's*, it poses an insoluble problem. The vulnerable part of the hero of the Trojan war is best described as an *Achilles heel*. Some possessives are so ugly that almost any lengths are justified to avoid them. *Congress's, Texas's* are examples.

Do not put apostrophes into decades: *the 1990s*, not *the 1990's*.

Remember, too, that phrases like *two weeks' time, six months' leave, a year's subscription, ten years' experience*, etc, also need apostrophes.

So do those involving *worth*, when it follows a sum, quantity or other measurement. After a figure or abbreviation, use a hyphen: *three months'-worth of imports, a manifesto's worth of insincerity.*

brackets (parentheses)

These can be used for short parenthetical explanations, or asides to the reader. Generally avoid putting long sentences in brackets. Do not overuse brackets as they can make for stuttering copy.

If a whole sentence is within brackets, put the full stop inside. Otherwise it goes outside.

Square brackets can be used for interpolations in direct quotations: *"Let them [the poor] eat cake."* To use ordinary brackets implies that the words inside them were part of the original. But square brackets are best dispensed with when you can shorten the quote instead: *She said that the poor could "eat cake".* Or rework it: *Of the poor, she said "Let them eat cake."*

colons

Remember that a colon should be used "to deliver the goods that have been invoiced in the preceding words" (Fowler). *They brought presents: gold, frankincense and oil at $100 a barrel.*

Use a colon before a whole quoted sentence, but not before a quotation that begins in mid-sentence. *She said: "It will never work."* He retorted that it had *"always worked before".*

commas

Remember that the comma signals a pause, but not everyone pauses in the same places.

British writers omit optional commas more often than American ones do. It is not usually necessary to put a comma after a short phrase at the start of a sentence, such as one specifying a time: *That night she took a tumble* or *On July 1st the country will hold elections.* The same goes for opening adverbs: *Suddenly he realised he was seeing unnecessary commas everywhere.*

But a breath, and so a comma, is needed after longer passages: *When day broke and she was able at last to see what had happened, she*

discovered she had fallen through the roof and into the Big Brother house.
A comma is also needed in shorter sentences where a *but* changes the
direction of travel: *He won the election, but with a reduced majority.*

Use two commas, or none at all, when inserting something in the
middle of a sentence. Thus, do not write: *Use two commas, or none at
all when inserting...* or *Use two commas or none at all, when inserting...*

Commas are essential (and often left out) after the names of
American states when these are written as though they were part of
an address: *Kansas City, Kansas, proves that even Kansas City needn't
always be Missourible* (Ogden Nash). *The University of California, Los
Angeles,* and other such campuses also need commas, which are a
defining part of their titles. So does *Mary, Queen of Scots,* in hers.

If the clause ends with a bracket, which is not uncommon (this
one does), the bracket should be followed by a comma.

Commas can alter the sense of a sentence. In *Mozart's 40th
symphony, in G minor,* the commas indicate that his 40th symphony
was written in G minor. Without commas, *Mozart's 40th symphony in
G minor* suggests he wrote 39 previous symphonies in G minor.

The Economist does not routinely use the serial comma—that is,
do not put a comma before *and* at the end of a sequence of items:
She ordered one bourbon, one scotch and one beer. But do use it when
the last item itself includes an *and*: *He ordered coffee, toast, and steak
and eggs.* Also use it when not doing so could introduce confused or
absurd readings, as in the apocryphal but delightful *I'd like to thank my
parents, Ayn Rand and God.* (These can also be re-ordered, but doing so
can change the emphasis or rhythm in an undesirable way.)

dashes

You can use em-dashes (long dashes) in pairs for a parenthesis, but
never more than one pair per sentence, ideally not more than one pair
per paragraph. You can use a single dash at the end of a sentence to
deliver a final flourish—sparingly.

"Use a dash to introduce an explanation, amplification,
paraphrase, particularisation or correction of what immediately
precedes it. Use it to gather up the subject of a long sentence. Use it to
introduce a paradoxical or whimsical ending to a sentence. Do not use
it as a punctuation maid-of-all-work" (Gowers).

full stops

Use them. They are usually preferable to colons, semi-colons and dashes. If a sentence is too long or complicated, break it up into two or more shorter ones.

(Note that *The Economist* does not use them with *Mr, Ms, Dr, eg, ie* and so on. See individual listings for those items if you are not sure.)

hyphens

There is no firm rule to help you decide which words are run together, hyphenated or left separate. Habits change over time, and American English is readier to accept compound words than British English. "*Week-end*" lost its hyphen in America in the 1950s, but kept it in Britain until the 1960s (and remains in use in French use of the anglicism).

"If you take hyphens seriously, you will surely go mad," says the style manual of the Oxford University Press. Hyphenation practices vary, making hard-and-fast rules elusive. Yet, maddening as they may be, you have to use hyphens. Take this headline from the newspaper in Pratt, Kansas: "*Students get first hand job experience*". Without a hyphen it is comically ambiguous. You may know something *first hand*, but it is *first-hand knowledge* when two words become a single modifier of a third word.

In general, try to avoid putting hyphens into words formed of one word and a short prefix, so *asexual, biplane, declassify, disfranchise, geopolitical, neoclassicism, neoliberal, neonatal, overeducated, preoccupied, preordained, prepay, realign, redirect, reopen, reorder, subhuman, underdone, upended, tetravalent*, etc.

But long words thus formed and unfamiliar combinations, especially if they would involve running several consonants together, may benefit from a hyphen, so *cross-reference* (though *crossfire*), *over-governed* and *under-secretary*. *Antidisestablishmentarianism* would, however, lose its point if hyphenated.

separating similar or identical letters
Because of the possibility that identical letters from two different syllables may be read as belonging to the same syllable, and because some simply look odd, separate them in such words as *book-keeping*

(but *bookseller*), *coat-tails*, *co-operate*, *unco-operative*, *pre-eminent*, *pre-empt* (but *predate*, *precondition*), *re-emerge*, *re-entry*, *re-use* (but *rearm*, *rearrange*, *reborn*, *repurchase*), *trans-ship*. Exceptions include *overreach*, *override*, *overrule*, *skiing*, *underrate*, *withhold*.

nouns formed from prepositional verbs
bail-out, *build-up*, *call-up*, *get-together*, *lay-off*, *pay-off*, *round-up*, *set-up*, *shake-up*, *stand-off* (but *fallout*, *handout*, *lockout*, *turnout*).

the quarters of the compass
north-east(ern), *south-east(ern)*, *south-west(ern)*, *north-west(ern)*, *mid-west(ern)*.

ethnic hybrids
Greek-Cypriot, *Irish-American*, etc, whether noun or adjective.

-makers, etc
A general, though not iron, rule for *makers*: if the prefix is of one or two syllables, attach it without a hyphen to form a single word, but if the prefix is of three or more syllables, introduce a hyphen. So *carmaker*, *chipmaker*, *peacemaker*, *marketmaker*, *troublemaker*, but *candlestick-maker*, *holiday-maker*, *tiramisu-maker*. *Policymaker* is an exception.

With other words ending -er that are similar to *maker* (*builder*, *dealer*, *driver*, *grower*, *owner*, *player*, *runner*, *seeker*, *trafficker*, *worker*, etc), the general rule should be to insert a hyphen. But some prefixes, especially those of one syllable, can be used to form single words (*coalminer*, *foxhunter*, *householder*, *landowner*, *metalworker*, *muckraker*, *nitpicker*, *shipbroker*, *steeplechaser*), and some combinations will be better left as two words (*insurance broker*, *crossword compiler*, *tuba player*).

See Chapter 10, Reference, for a full list of words *The Economist* hyphenates, closes up and leaves separated.

inverted commas (quotation marks)

Use single ones only for quotations within quotations. Thus: *"When I say 'punctual', I mean five minutes early," said the assistant on the phone.*

For the relative placing of quotation marks and punctuation, the rule is straightforward: if the quoted material is a full sentence, the punctuation goes inside. *"I'm sorry I was late," he said.*

If the material in inverted commas is not a full sentence, the punctuation goes outside. *The interviewer muttered that it was "no problem", but sat down with a face that indicated that it was indeed a problem.*

When a quotation is broken off and resumed after such words as he said, ask yourself whether it would naturally have had any punctuation at the point where it is broken off. If the answer is yes, a comma is placed within the quotation marks to represent this. Thus, *"If you have quite composed yourself," he said, "let's begin."*

But if the words to be quoted are continuous, without punctuation at the point where they are broken, the comma should be outside the inverted commas. Thus, *"I assure you", he stuttered, "that this has never happened before."*

A quotation within a sentence needs to be preceded by a comma, a colon, or a word such as *that* (or *if, because, whether,* etc), if the quotation is an entire sentence. The first quoted word should also have an initial capital. Thus *Unimpressed, he responded, "Make sure that it doesn't become a habit."* If the words quoted are not an entire sentence, neither comma nor capital is needed: *Unimpressed, he responded that it shouldn't "become a habit".*

If you want to quote a full sentence and precede it with the word *that, because,* etc, no comma is needed before the inverted commas, but the first quoted word still needs a capital: *He briskly replied that "Once I have the job, it certainly won't."*

question marks

Except in sentences that include a question in inverted commas, question marks always come at the end of the sentence. *Where could he get a bite, he wondered?*

semi-colons

Semi-colons should be used to mark a pause longer than a comma and shorter than a full stop. Don't overdo them.

Use them where any items in a list themselves contain commas. Thus *They agreed on only three points: the ceasefire should be immediate; it should be internationally supervised, preferably by the AU; and a peace conference should be held, either in Geneva or in Ouagadougou.*

Figures

Never start a sentence with a figure; write the number in words instead.

In general, though, use figures for numerals from 11 upwards:

first to tenth centuries
20th century, 21st century
20th-century ideas
in 100 years
a 29-year-old man
a man in his 20s
20th anniversary
two and a half years later
40-something, 40-fold, the 1940s (etc), but *four-fold*

The *Thirty Years War* is an exception.

Use figures, too, for all numerals that include a *decimal point* (eg, 4.25). Figures may also be appropriate for *fractions*, if the context is either technical or precise, or both (eg, *Though the poll's figures were supposed to be accurate to within 1%, his lead of 4¼ points turned out on election day to be minus 3½*). Where precision is less important but it is nonetheless impossible to shoot off the fraction, words may look better: *Though the animal was sold as a two-year-old, it turned out to be two and a half times that.*

Fractions should be hyphenated (*one-half, three-quarters*, etc) and, unless they are attached to whole numbers (8½, 29¾), spelled out in words, even when the figures are higher than ten: *He left a tenth of his estate to his wife, a twentieth to the church and a thirtieth to charity.*

Do not compare a fraction with a *decimal* (so avoid *The rate fell from 3¼% to 3.1%*).

Fractions may be more precise than *decimals* (*3.33* neglects an infinity of figures that are included in 1/3), but your readers probably will not think so. You should therefore use fractions for rough figures (*A hectare is about 2½ acres*) and decimals for more exact ones: *The retail price index is rising at an annual rate of 10.6%*. But treat all numbers with respect. That usually means resisting the precision of more than one decimal place, and generally favouring rounding off.

Use words for simple numerals from one to ten, except: in references to pages; in percentages (eg, *4%*); and in sets of numerals, some of which are higher than ten, eg, *children between 8 and 12*. It is occasionally permissible to use words rather than numbers when referring to a rough or rhetorical figure (such as *a thousand curses*).

A *billion* is a thousand million, a *trillion* a thousand billion, a *quadrillion* a thousand trillion.

Use *5,000-6,000, 5-6%, 5m-6m* (not *5-6m*) and *5bn-6bn*. But *sales rose from 5m to 6m* (not *5m-6m*); *estimates ranged between 5m and 6m* (not *5m-6m*).

$5,000-6,000 (not *$5,000-$6,000* or *$5-6,000*)
$5m-6m (not *$5m-$6m*)
$5bn-6bn (not *$5-6bn*)

Where *to* is being used as part of a *ratio*, it is usually best to spell everything out without dashes or hyphens. Thus *They decided, by nine votes to two, to put the matter to the assembly, which voted, 27 to 19, to insist that the ratio of vodka to tomato juice in a bloody mary should be at least one to three, though the odds of this being so in most bars were put at no better than 11 to 4*. Where a ratio is being used adjectivally, figures and hyphens may be used, but only if one of the figures is greater than ten: thus *a 50-20 vote, a 19-9 vote*. Otherwise, spell out the figures and use *to*: *a two-to-one vote, a ten-to-one probability*.

Do not use a hyphen in place of *to* except with figures: *He received a sentence of 15-20 years in jail* but *He promised to escape within three to four weeks*.

With figures, use *a person* or *per person*, *a year* or *per year*, not *per caput, per capita* or *per annum*.

In most non-American contexts, use metric units: prefer *hectares* to *acres*, *kilometres* (or *km*) to *miles*, *metres* to *yards*, *litres* to *gallons*, *kilos* to *lb*, *tonnes* to *tons*, etc. For an American audience, use the measurements more familiar to Americans (though remember that American pints, quarts, gallons, etc, are smaller than imperial ones). Regardless of which you choose, you should give an equivalent, on first use, in the other units: *It was hoped that after improvements to the engine the car would give 20km to the litre (47 miles per American gallon), compared with its present average of 15km per litre.*

Remember that *petrol* is sold in imperial gallons in very few countries now. In America it is sold in American gallons; in most other places it is sold in litres.

Use the sign % instead of *per cent*. But write *percentage*, not %age (though in most contexts *proportion* or *share* is preferable).

A fall from 4% to 2% is a drop of two percentage points, or of 50%, but not of 2%.

Do not use pointlessly exact or unknowable statistics in an attempt to lend weight to your writing, as in *178,000 manganese nodules lie at the bottom of the Sargasso Sea.* And, even worse, do not disguise ignorance by qualifying figures with the words *up to*, as advertisers do when claiming their product *lasts up to 80% longer.*

Headings and captions

Headings and captions set the tone of your writing: they are more read than anything else. Use them, therefore, to draw readers in, not to repel them. That means wit (where appropriate), not bad puns; sharpness (ditto), not familiarity (call people by their last names, not their first names); originality, not clichés.

Writers and editors, having laboured over their writing, are too often ready to yank a well-known catchphrase, or the title of a film or song, from the front of their minds without giving the matter any more thought. If you find yourself reaching for any of the following, think again:

Anything *2.0*; anything *redux*; *back to the future*; *bridges* (or anything else) *too far*; *deal or no deal*; *empires striking back*; *French connections*; *Italian jobs*; *F-words*; *flavours of the month*; *hearts and minds*; *mind the gap*; *new kids on the block*; *perfect storms*; *$64,000 questions*; *shaken, not stirred*; *somebody rules, OK*; *southern discomfort*; *thirty-somethings*; *windows of opportunity*; *where's the beef?*; *could do better* (a favourite with education stories); *taxing times* (tax stories).

In 2004 an *Economist* reader wrote:

SIR - Your newspaper this week contains headlines derived from the following film titles: "As Good As It Gets", "Face-Off", "From Russia With Love", "The Man Who Planted Trees", "Up Close and Personal" and "The Way of the Warrior". Also employed are "The Iceman Cometh", "Measure for Measure", "The Tyger" and "War and Peace" – to say nothing of the old stalwart, "Howard's Way".

Is this a competition, or do your sub-editors need to get out more?

Be warned.
(See also Chapter 2 on metaphors and journalese.)

Abbreviations

Unless an abbreviation or acronym is so familiar that it is used more often than the full form (eg, *AIDS*, *BBC*, *CIA*, *EU*, *FBI*, *HIV*, *IMF*, *NATO*, *NGO*, *OECD*, *UN*, *UNESCO*), or unless the full form would provide little illumination (eg, *AWACS*, *DNA*), write the words in full on first appearance: thus, *Trades Union Congress* (not *TUC*). If in doubt about its familiarity, explain what the organisation does. After the first mention, try not to repeat the abbreviation too often; so write *the agency* rather than *the IAEA*, *the party* rather than *the KMT*, to avoid spattering the page with capital letters. Do not give the initials of an organisation on first mention if it is not referred to again. This clutters both the page and the brain.

If an abbreviation can be pronounced (eg, *NATO*, *UNESCO*), it does not generally require the definite article. Other organisations, except companies, should usually be preceded by *the* (*the BBC*, *the KGB*, *the NHS* and *the UNHCR*).

Abbreviations that can be pronounced and are composed of bits of words rather than just initials should be spelt out in upper and lower case: *Cocom*, *Frelimo*, *Kfor*, *Legco*, *Mercosur*, *Nepad*, *Renamo*, *Sfor*, *Unicef*, *Unisom*, *Unprofor*, *Seals* (American navy), *Trips* (trade-related aspects of intellectual-property rights). There is generally no need for more than one capital letter per word, unless the word is a proper name: *ConsGold*, *KwaZulu*, *McKay*, *MiG*.

Do not shorten *streets*, *avenues*, etc, in postal addresses, and be sure to include all necessary commas. *The president lives at 1600 Pennsylvania Avenue, Washington, DC, and seems to enjoy it.*

Do not abbreviate *miles* (though *mph* is all right), *nautical miles, yards, feet, inches, metres, gallons, acres, hectares, tonnes, tons, pints, ounces, bits, bytes, hertz* and multiples—*terabytes, megahertz,* etc (except in charts, where abbreviation is permissible).

But *kilograms* (not *kilogrammes*) and *kilometres* can be shortened to *kg* (or *kilos*) and *km*. Miles per hour are *mph* and kilometres per hour are *kph*.

Use *m* for *million, bn* for *billion* and *trn* for *trillion*.

Use lower case for *kg, km, lb* (never *lbs*), *mph* and other measures, and for *ie* and *eg*, which should both be followed by commas. When used with figures, these lower-case abbreviations should follow immediately, with no space (*11am, 4.30pm, 15kg, 35mm, 100mph, 78rpm*), as should AD and BC (*76AD, 55BC*). Two abbreviations together, however, must be separated: *60m b/d.*

Scientific units that are named after people are not capitalised when written out in full: *watt, joule, hertz, sievert,* etc.

Multiples and fractional units are listed below, with their prefix spelled out (*kilo-*), their multiple or fraction (thousand) and their abbreviation (*k*). Spell out peta-, exa-, micro-, pico- and femto- units, as these do not have prefixes familiar to most readers.

kilo- (thousand) *k*
mega- (million) M
giga- (billion) G
tera- (trillion) T
peta- (10^{15})
exa- (10^{18})

Fractions are formed with:

milli- (thousandth) *m*
micro- (millionth)
nano- (billionth) *n*
pico-
femto-

We write a millionth of a metre as a *micron*, not a *micrometre*.

Initials in people's names, or in companies named after them, take full stops (with a space between initials and name, but not between initials). Thus *A.D. Miller*, *F.W. de Klerk*. In general, follow the practice preferred by people, companies and organisations in writing their own names.

When the Latin name of a genus is shortened to a single initial on second mention (eg, *H. sapiens*), it too should be followed by a full stop. (See Latin names, p. 114.)

Do not use *Prof* (*Professor*) or *Sen* (*Senator*).

Ampersands should be used

1. when they are part of the name of a company (eg, *AT&T*, *Pratt & Whitney*);
2. for such things as constituencies where two names are linked to form one unit (eg, *The area thus became the Pakistani province of Kashmir and the Indian state of Jammu & Kashmir*);
3. in *R&D* and *S&L*.

Remember, too, that the *D* of *DAB* stands for digital, so do not write *DAB digital radio*. Similarly, the *V* of *HIV* stands for virus, so do not write *HIV virus*.

Members of Parliament are *MPs*: of the *Scottish Parliament*, *MSPs*; and of the *European Parliament*, *MEPs*. Members of the Welsh Senedd are *MSs*.

Spell out in full (and lower case) *junior* and *senior* after a name: *Donald Trump junior*, *Hank Williams senior*.

Dates

Be consistent. *The Economist* uses *month, day, year*, in that order, with no commas:

July 5th	*1996-99*
Monday July 5th	*2002-05*
July 5th 2015	*1998-2003*
July 27th-August 3rd 2015	*1990s*
July 2022	

Do not write *on June 10th-14th*, but *between June 10th and 14th*. If, say, ministers are to meet over two days, write *on December 14th and 15th*.

Avoid *last week*, *next week* and *this week*; *last month*, *next month*. Give the date. And avoid *this year*, *next year*, etc, in articles written close to the turn of the year.

For global events or those not tied to a single place, avoid references to *summer*, *winter*, etc, which are different depending on the hemisphere. (When writing about a single country, mentioning seasons is acceptable, but be more precise if you can.)

Dates that require AD or BC should be set as one unhyphenated word (*76AD, 55BC*).

Currencies

Apart from those currencies that are written out in full (see below), write the abbreviation followed by the number. Currencies are not set in small capitals unless they occur as words in text without figures attached: *"Out went the D-mark, in came the euro."*

Britain

pound, abbreviated as £
pence, abbreviated as *p*
1p, 2p, 3p, etc, to *99p* (not *£0.99*)
£6 (not *£6.00*), *£6.47*
£5,000-6,000 (not *£5,000-£6,000*)

America

dollar, abbreviated as *$*, will do generally; *US$* only if there is a mixture of dollar currencies (see below)
cents, spell out, unless part of a larger number: *$4.99*

other dollar currencies

A$	Australian dollars	NT$	Taiwanese dollars
C$	Canadian dollars	NZ$	New Zealand dollars
HK$	Hong Kong dollars	S$	Singaporean dollars
M$	Malaysian dollars	Z$	Zimbabwean dollars

Europe

euro, plural *euros*, abbreviated as €
cents, spell out, unless part of a larger number
€10, €10.75
DM, BFr, drachmas, FFr, Italian lire, IR£ (punts), markkas, Asch, Ptas
and others that have been replaced may turn up in historical
references.
DKr Danish krone (plural kroner)
IKr Icelandic krona (plural kronur)
NKr Norwegian krone (plural kroner)
SFr Swiss franc, SFr1m (not 1m Swiss francs)
SKr Swedish krona (plural kronor)

Sums in all other currencies are written in full, with the number first.

Brazil, real, 100m reais
China, yuan, 100m yuan (not renminbi) (see below)
India, rupee, 100m rupees
Nigeria, naira, 100m naira
peso currencies, 100m pesos
South Africa, rand, 100m rand (not rands)
Turkey, Turkish lira, 100m liras
But Japan, yen ¥, ¥1,000 (not 1,000 yen)
Russia has roubles, not rubles.
Venezuela has the bolívar, plural bolívares.

China

Use *yuan*, even though this means simply *money*. (*Renminbi*, which
means *the people's currency*, describes the yuan in the same way that
sterling describes the pound, but is unnecessary.)

Titles (people)

The overriding principle is to treat people with respect. That usually
means giving them the title they themselves adopt. But our first goal
is clarity. Some titles are misleading (all Italian graduates are *Dr*), and
we do not want to confuse. The second goal is readability; Germans

may pile up titles like *Herr Professor Doktor Schmidt* but in English, simplicity trumps formality.

Do not use *Mr, Ms* or *Dr* on first mention, even in the main text (and never in titles, captions or rubrics). Plain *Barack Obama* or *David Cameron* will do. But thereafter the names of all living people should be preceded by *Mr, Ms* or some other title.

Ms is the default for a woman who is not publicly known to prefer *Miss* or *Mrs*.

academic titles

Use *Dr* with those who hold a doctorate, work as a university scholar or researcher and are in your copy because of their expertise. Other public figures with doctorates should be *Mr* or *Ms*.

Dr is also used on second mention for practising medical doctors (though by tradition, surgeons in Britain use *Mr, Ms, Mrs*, etc, instead).

Use *Professor* (not *Prof*) only with those of that rank in Britain or the rank of full professor in America and elsewhere, since American *assistant* and *associate professors* are equivalent to *lecturer*, reader, etc, in Britain.

clerical titles

Ordained clerics should be given their proper titles, though not their full honorifics (no need for *His Holiness, His Eminence*, the *Right Reverend*, etc).

In some denominations, clergy continue to use their secular surnames. Others virtually abandon their surnames and use only their titular first name, which may be different from that on their birth certificate.

In Catholicism, the pope goes only by the first name he has chosen, eg, *Pope Francis*, who can be simply *Francis* at second reference. For cardinals, archbishops and bishops (overlapping categories), the first mention should have the title before both names: *Cardinal Pietro Parolin*. On second mention use the title plus the surname: *Cardinal Parolin, Archbishop Martin, Bishop Smith*. In cases where a cardinal is also an archbishop, use *Cardinal*. For rank-and-file priests, it is *Father Smith* on second reference.

In Orthodox and Coptic Christianity surnames are dropped, and titular first names rule. Thus *Patriarch Kirill* (of Moscow), *Patriarch Bartholomew* (of Constantinople), *Archbishop Dimitrios* (the former Orthodox prelate for North America), *Pope Shenouda* (Coptic prelate in Egypt), etc. For ordinary priests it is both names on first mention, then *Father* plus the first name, eg, *Father Alexander*, on second mention. (Do not use the surname.)

For Anglicans, Episcopalians and other reformed churches with bishops (eg, Lutherans), use *Archbishop Smith* or *Bishop Smith* at second reference. For rank-and-file clergy, *Mr*, *Ms* or *Mrs* is best. That also goes for those nonconformist Protestants who generally have no bishops and play down the clergy's separateness: it is *Mr*, *Ms* or *Mrs* at second reference.

Other religious leaders should be given an appropriate title if they use one, and it should be repeated on second and subsequent mentions, so, *Ayatollah Hossein-Ali Montazeri (Ayatollah Montazeri)*, *Rabbi Lionel Bloom (Rabbi Bloom)*, *Sri Sri Ravi Shankar (Sri Sri Ravi Shankar)*, etc.

military titles

On first mention of military officers, give their full rank and both names, so *Lieutenant Commander Pete Mitchell says that...*

On second mention, various ranks are shortened for use with a surname only. For example

Lieutenant General (John Jones)	*General (Jones)*
Major General	*General*
Brigadier General (not in use in Britain)	*General*
Lieutenant Colonel	*Colonel*
Lieutenant Commander	*Commander*
Vice Admiral	*Admiral*
Rear Admiral	*Admiral*
1st Lieutenant	*Lieutenant*
2nd Lieutenant	*Lieutenant*

When quoting retired senior military personnel in their capacity as military experts, on first mention you may write *Eric Springer, a retired air force colonel, says...* On subsequent mention, he is still

Colonel Springer. Always use *retired*. Calling someone a *former general* or *ex-admiral* implies they have been stripped of their rank, usually for wrongdoing.

If someone has notably turned in their uniform to take a civilian job, as Colin Powell did to become secretary of state, they become *Mr* or *Ms*.

noble titles, knighthoods, etc

On first mention all viscounts, earls, marquesses, dukes, etc, should be given their titles (shorn of *Right Honourables*, etc). Thereafter they can be plain *Lord* (except for dukes). *Barons*, a category that includes all life peers, can always be called *Lord*. Those like *Norman Foster* may be called by these, their familiar names, on first mention. After that, they should be given their titles: *Lord Foster* (never *Lord Norman Foster*: that would imply he was the son of a marquess or a duke). Life peeresses may be called *Lady*, not *Baroness*, just as barons are called *Lord*.

The full names of knights and dames should be spelled out on first mention: *Dame Firstname Lastname*. Thereafter they become *Sir Firstnameonly* or *Dame Firstnameonly*. Note that some people choose not to use their titles. If you know this to be the case, Mr or Ms Lastname is fine.

job titles

Governor X, President Y, Chancellor Z may be *Mr* or *Ms* on second mention. If using the title on first mention, give the first name also: *President Joe Biden*.

Except those above like governor and chancellor, other job titles should not be joined directly to names. Avoid *Prime Minister Boris Johnson, Finance Minister Christian Lindner, Enlargement Commissioner Olli Rehn*. It is *Christian Lindner, the finance minister*....

That also goes for business titles, which are undergoing rapid inflation (no *chief happiness officer Sven Svensen*). Except for unusually senior titles like *chief executive* and a few others, most need not even be mentioned. Instead, if needed, describe what the person does for the company. Those titles that must be mentioned go after the name: *Hans Hansen, the chief financial officer*....

In most cases omit middle initials. Nobody will imagine that the *Lyndon Johnson* you are writing about is *Lyndon A. Johnson* or *Lyndon C. Johnson*. An exception is the helpful distinction between *George W. Bush* (not properly a *junior*) and his father, *George H.W. Bush*.

Some titles serve as names, and therefore have initial capitals, though they also serve as descriptions: the *Archbishop of Canterbury*, the *Emir of Kuwait*, the *Shah of Iran*. If you want to describe the office rather than the individual, use lower case: *The next archbishop of Canterbury will be a woman*. Use lower case, too, in references simply to *the archbishop, the emir, the shah*: *The Duchess of Scunthorpe was in her finery, but the duke wore jeans*.

exceptions

Sometimes titles (eg, knighthoods) can be dispensed with for athletes and pop stars, if they would seem more ridiculous than dignified. No titles for the dead, except those whom you are writing about because they have just died. For obituaries, therefore, titles are required. *Dr Johnson* and *Mr Gladstone* are also permissible.

Avoid nicknames and diminutives unless the person is always known (or prefers to be known) by one: *Joe Biden, Tony Blair, Dick Cheney, Newt Gingrich*.

Capitals

Use capitals to avoid confusion, especially with no (and therefore yes). *In Bergen no votes predominated* suggests a stalemate, whereas *In Bergen No votes predominated* suggests a triumph of noes over yeses. In most contexts, though, *yes* and *no* should be lower case: "The answer was no." Also capitalise *In* and *Out* or *Leave* and *Remain* (as in the EU referendum campaign).

8

What's in a name: people, organisations and places around the world

The Economist writes about people, places, works of art and more from places around the world. Doing so requires many difficult decisions about spelling (in the case of non-Latin alphabets rendered into our own), capitalisations, place names (which are highly contested in many places), given and family names, and much more. It is impossible to please everyone all of the time but this chapter contains the decisions made over many years in the effort to balance consistency, accuracy, respect and readability.

Capitalised words

organisations

Organisations, ministries, departments, treaties, acts, etc, generally take upper case when their full name (or something pretty close to it, eg, *State Department*) is used. Thus, *European Commission, Forestry Commission, Arab League, Amnesty International, the Scottish Parliament (the parliament), the Welsh Assembly (the assembly), the Household Cavalry, Ministry of Defence, Department for Environment, Food and Rural Affairs (DEFRA), Treasury, Metropolitan Police, High Court, Supreme Court, Court of Appeal, 5th Circuit Court of Appeals* (but *6th congressional district*), *Central Committee, Politburo, Oxford University, the New York Stock Exchange, Treaty of Rome, the Health and Safety at Work Act*, etc.

So too *the House of Commons, House of Lords, House of*

Representatives, *St Paul's Cathedral* (the cathedral), *Bank of England* (the bank), *Department of State* (the department), *World Bank* (the bank).

But organisations, committees, commissions, special groups, etc, that are either impermanent, ad hoc, local or relatively insignificant should be lower case. Thus: *the subcommittee on journalists' rights of the National Executive Committee of the Labour Party, the international economic subcommittee of the Senate Foreign Relations Committee, the Oxford University bowls club, Market Blandings rural district council.*

Use lower case for rough descriptions (*the safety act*, the *American health department*, the *French parliament*, as distinct from its *National Assembly*). If you are not sure whether the English translation of a foreign name is exact or not, assume it is rough and use lower case.

Congress and *Parliament* are upper case, unless parliament is used not to describe the institution but the period of time for which it sits (so *This bill will not be brought forward until the next parliament*). However, give a capital only to those parliaments that explicitly call themselves *Parliament*, as, eg, *Australia's*, *Britain's*, *Canada's* and *Malaysia's* do.

Give *Congress* or a *Supreme Court* its capital only where the name is English; the many *congresses* in Latin America are lower case.

Congressional and *parliamentary* are lower case, as is the *opposition*, even when used in the sense of *his majesty's loyal opposition*. The *government*, the *administration* and the *cabinet* are always lower case. In America acts given the names of their sponsors (eg, *Glass-Steagall*, *Helms-Burton*, *Sarbanes-Oxley*) are always rough descriptions and so take a lower-case *act*.

Parliament (the institution). Do not confuse one part of a parliament with the whole thing. The *Dail* is only the lower house of Ireland's parliament, as the *Duma* is of Russia's and the *Lok Sabha* is of India's.

The full name of political parties is upper case, including the word *party*: *Republican Party, Labour Party*. But note that some parties, such as Greece's *New Democracy*, India's *Congress*, Indonesia's *Golkar*, Turkey's *Justice and Development*, etc, do not have *party* as part of their names. It should therefore be lower case. In Italy it is the *Northern League* on first mention, then the *League*.

Note, too, that usually only people are *Democrats*, *Christian Democrats*, *Liberal Democrats* or *Social Democrats*; their parties, policies, candidates, committees, etc, are *Democratic*, *Christian Democratic*, *Liberal Democratic* or *Social Democratic* (although a committee may be *Democrat-controlled*). The exceptions are Britain's *Liberal Democrat Party* and Thailand's *Democrat Party*.

When referring to a specific party, write *Labour*, the *Republican nominee*, a prominent *Liberal*, etc, but use lower case in looser references to *liberals*, *conservatism*, *communists*, etc. *Tories* are upper case. *Tea Party* is spelt thus.

A political, economic or religious label formed from a proper name—eg, *Gaullism*, *Paisleyite*, *Leninist*, *Napoleonic*, *Wilsonian*, *Jacobite*, *Luddite*, *Marxist*, *Hobbesian*, *Thatcherism*, *Christian*, *Buddhism*, *Hindu*, *Islamic*, *Maronite*, *Finlandisation*—should have a capital.

Schools of painting or literature (*Cubism*, *Expressionism*, *Impressionism*, *Fauvism*, *Modernism*, etc) are upper case, as are their adjectives and their practitioners (*Modernists*, *Romantics*).

In finance and government there are particular exceptions to the general rule of initial caps for full names, lower case for informal ones. Use caps for the *World Bank* and the *Fed* (after first spelling it out as the *Federal Reserve*), although these are shortened, informal names. The *Bank of England* and its foreign equivalents have initial caps when named formally and separately, but collectively they are central banks in lower case (except those like Brazil's, Ireland's and Venezuela's, which are actually named the *Central Bank*).

Deutschmarks are still known just as *D-marks*, even though all references are historical. *Treasury bonds* issued by America's Treasury should be upper case; *treasury bills* (or *bonds*) of a general kind should be lower case. Avoid *T-bonds* and *t-bills*.

After first mention, the *House of Commons* (or *Lords*, or *Representatives*) becomes the *House*, and the *World Bank* and *Bank of England* become the *bank*, just as the *IMF* may become the *fund*. Organisations with unusual or misleading names, such as the *African National Congress* and *Civic Forum*, may become the *Congress* and the *Forum* on second and subsequent mentions. But most other organisations—agencies, banks, commissions (including the *European Commission* and the *European Union*), etc—take lower case when referred to incompletely on second mention.

places

Use upper case for definite geographical places, regions, areas and countries (*The Hague, Transylvania, Germany*), and for vague but recognised political or geographical areas: *the Middle East, South Atlantic, East Asia* (not *the Far East*), *the West* (as in the decline of the West; adjective, *Western*), *the Persian Gulf, the North Atlantic, South-East Asia, the Midlands, Central America, the West Country.*

Lower case for *east, west, north, south* (eg, *north Africa, west Africa, eastern Europe*) except when part of a name (*North Korea, South Africa, West End*) or part of a thinking group (*the South, the Midwest, the West*), but lower case for vaguer areas such as the American north-east, north-west, south-east, south-west, or Russia's far east. *The Highlands* (of Scotland), *the Midlands* (of England). If you are, say, comparing regions some of which would normally be upper case and some lower case, and it would look odd to leave them that way, put them all lower case: *House prices in the north-east and the south are rising faster than those in the mid-west and the south-west.* (In these cases adjectives are always lower case: midwestern, southern.)

Europe's divisions are no longer neatly political, and are now geographically imprecise, so use lower case for *central, eastern* and *western Europe*. But *North, Central* and *South America* are clearly defined areas, so should be given capitals, as should *Central, South, East* and *South-East Asia*.

We have adopted local spellings for some Spanish places: *Andalucía*, not *Andalusia* (the adjective *Andalucian* should have no accent); *Zaragoza*, not *Saragossa*. Some places get their regional spellings: *A Coruña*, not *La Coruña*. That said, *Catalonia, Navarre* and *Castile* remain in the anglicised form. But *Castile* becomes *Castilla y León* and *Castilla-La Mancha* in the names of the two official regions.

The *Basque country* (or *region*) is ill defined and contentious, and may include parts of both France and Spain. Lower case for *country* (or *region* or *lands*) when you mean the cultural area. Use *Basque Country* only for the smaller Spanish region that is officially so named, and be clear in your copy if that is what you mean.

Use *West Germany* (*West Berlin*) and *East Germany* (*East Berlin*) only in historical references. They are now *west* or *western Germany* (*Berlin*) and *east* or *eastern Germany* (*eastern Berlin*).

South Africa is a country; *southern, central, east, west* and *north Africa* are regions.

The *third world* (another term now happily confined to history, especially as the communist second world has disappeared) is lower case.

Use capitals for particular buildings even if the name is not strictly accurate (eg, the *Foreign Office*).

Capitalise *Sea, Ocean, River*, etc, if it is always part of the name. Hence *South China Sea, Arctic Ocean, Snake River, Permian Basin, Pearl River Delta, Malacca Straits*. Use upper case too in the rare cases where the name comes after the feature: *River Thames, River Jordan*. Use lower case, and preferably omit, where the feature is not an essential part of the name: the *Atlantic*, the *Mississippi*, the *Euphrates*, the *Ganges*. *The English Channel* (*the channel* on second mention). Note that American counties are part of the name (*Madison County*).

Note that *City* is sometimes an integral part of a name, as in *Dodge City, Kansas City, Quezon City, Oklahoma City, Salt Lake City*, and is therefore upper case. If *city* is not integral to the name, but is required for some reason (eg, to differentiate the town from a state or country of the same name), it should be lower case. Thus *Gaza city, Guatemala city, Ho Chi Minh city, Kuwait city, Mexico city, Panama city* and *Quebec city*. But note: *New York City*.

If in doubt use lower case (*the sunbelt*).

food and drink

Lower case should be used for most common dishes and familiar wines, cheeses, grape varieties, etc. Thus *bombay duck, bordeaux, barolo, burgundy, champagne, chardonnay, cheddar, chicken kiev, dim sum, emmental, gorgonzola, hock, merlot, moselle, parmesan, pinotage, primitivo, rioja, russian salad, syrah, vindaloo, zinfandel*. But the proper names of particular wines or *appellations* take upper case (*Cheval Blanc, Lafite, Marqués de Riscal*), as do some foods and drinks that would look odd lower case, eg, *Parma ham, Scotch whisky*.

plants

For informal names of plants and flowers that are part of the language, lower case is fine: *chrysanthemum, buttercup, daisy, delphinium, oleander*, etc. But where part of the name is a proper name, some capitals may be necessary: *pride of India, grass of Parnassus, Spanish moss*, etc.

For the scientific names of animals, plants, etc, see Latin names, p. 114.

trade names

Companies try to avoid having their trademarks used as a generic name for the product, as this can lead to "genericide": the loss of their brand distinctiveness, and possibly even the loss of their trademark. They may hassle you to capitalise their names and use them only for their branded products. But they cannot force you to do so.

That said, distinctive, recent trademarks should be given their capitals, whether *Google* or *Photoshop*; use another phrase ("search online" instead of the verb *to Google*) if you mean the generic. A *Hoover* still gets its capital, as do *Teflon* and *Valium*. But *aspirin, heroin, escalator* and many other former trademarks have long been generic. In the middle are *Dumpster, Frisbee* and the like. They may sound like generics but their trademarks are still held. Capitalise them where this would not look absurd.

Company names

The best way to avoid errors when spelling company names is to look them up on the firms' own websites. (Occasionally, firms themselves use multiple versions of their name; when in doubt, use the one favoured by the investor-relations portion of a corporate site.)

Many company names are silly; few are so ridiculous that they should be changed unilaterally. If a firm's name is all upper case, like *COSTCO* or *IKEA*, follow suit; similarly, when a stray capital appears in the middle of a name, like *eBay* or *BlackRock*. If you are starting a sentence with a company that eschews capitals, capitalise (*"EBay is a fine name."*) But if a firm styles its name as entirely lower case, cap the first letter, so *Thyssenkrupp*, not *thyssenkrupp*, even if not at the beginning of a sentence.

Think harder about mimicking whimsical characters in company names: the exclamation mark in *Yahoo!*, a one-time internet icon, deserved to be dropped. There is usually no need to include suffixes like *Inc*, *plc*, *Ltd*, *S.A.* and so on.

A short and highly selective list of names that often cause problems:

Airbnb (not AirBnB)
Anheuser-Busch InBev
AstraZeneca
Bernstein (though its full name is AllianceBernstein)
BioNTech
BlackRock (but *Blackstone*)
Bouygues
ByteDance
Citigroup
ConocoPhillips
ExxonMobil (not just Exxon, even on second mention)
Hewlett-Packard split itself in two, so either *HP* or *Hewlett Packard Enterprise*
Intesa Sanpaolo
Johnson & Johnson (then *J&J*)
JPMorgan Chase
L'Oréal
Lloyd's (the insurance market)
Lloyds Banking Group
McDonald's
Nasdaq (the exchange)
NASDAQ (the index, in small capitals)
Nvidia
PepsiCo
PitchBook
PwC
Saudi Aramco (on first mention; thereafter, *Aramco*)
Shell (no longer Royal Dutch Shell even on first mention, and no longer an Anglo-Dutch oil giant, just *British*)
S&P Global (not Standard & Poor's)
Société Générale
SoftBank
SpaceX (ordinary capital X, not small cap)

Stellantis
Telefónica
Thyssenkrupp
TotalEnergies (not Total)
UniCredit
Walmart

Countries and their inhabitants

In most contexts favour simplicity over precision. So use *Britain* rather than *Great Britain* or the *United Kingdom*, and *America* rather than the *United States*. "In all pointed sentences, some degree of accuracy must be sacrificed to conciseness" (Dr Johnson).

Sometimes, however, it may be important to be precise. Remember therefore that *Great Britain* consists of *England*, *Scotland* and *Wales*, which together with *Northern Ireland* make up the *United Kingdom*. (Be careful with *Ulster*, which strictly includes three counties in the republic of *Ireland*)

Holland, though a nice, short, familiar name, is strictly only two of the 12 provinces that make up *the Netherlands*, and the *Dutch* are increasingly indignant about misuse of the shorter name. So use *the Netherlands*.

Ireland is simply *Ireland*. Although it is a republic, it is not formally the Republic of Ireland. Neither is it, in English, Eire. *North* and *south* should not have capitals in the Irish context.

Remember too that, although it is usually all right to talk about the inhabitants of the United States as *Americans*, the term also applies to everyone from Canada to Cape Horn. In a context where other North, Central or South American countries are mentioned, you should write *United States* rather than America or American, and it may even be necessary to write *United States citizens*.

Europe and *Europeans* may sometimes be used as shorthand for citizens of countries of the European Union, but be careful: there are plenty of other Europeans too.

Scandinavia is Denmark, Norway and Sweden. Iceland is culturally and linguistically related, but not part of the region. And Finland, with its utterly unrelated language, is most definitely not *Scandinavian*. Denmark, Iceland, Norway, Sweden and Finland make up the *Nordic countries*.

Where countries have made it clear that they wish to be called by a new (or an old) name, respect their requests. Thus *Eswatini* (formerly Swaziland), *Myanmar, Burkina Faso, Congo, Sri Lanka, Thailand, Zimbabwe*, etc.

The state is called *North Macedonia* but its people are *Macedonians*, not North Macedonians. *Macedonian* is the correct adjective for anything connected to identity.

Myanmar has no easy adjective, so *Burmese* is acceptable for the people of *Myanmar* in general. But note that the main ethnic group in Myanmar is the *Burmans*. The Kachin and Karen, among others, are Burmese but not Burman.

The *Pashtun* are the people. They speak *Pashto*.

Roma: this is the name of the people. Their language is *Romany*. *Gypsy* has fallen from favour, as it is based on a misconception (that they came from Egypt) and is not what most call themselves. But some groups (eg, Spain's) do call themselves by the local equivalent (gitanos). You may use *gypsies* in such cases, with care.

Former Soviet republics that are now independent countries include:

Belarus (not Belorussia), *Belarusian* (not Belarussian)
Kazakhstan
Kyrgyzstan (note spelling)
Moldova (not Moldavia)
Tajikistan
Turkmenistan (see *Turk, Turkic, Turkmen*, etc, on p. 177)

The people of *Niger* should usually be referred to as *the people* (or *inhabitants*) *of Niger*: clumsy, but better than calling them Nigerians. In extremis, they may be *Nigeriens*.

Some cities have inhabitants with odd names, at least to outsiders:

Glasgow: *Glaswegians*
Liverpool: *Liverpudlians*
Manchester: *Mancunians*
Mumbai: *Mumbaikars*
Naples: *Neapolitans*
Rio de Janeiro: *Cariocas*
São Paulo: *Paulistanos* (*Paulistas* come from São Paulo state)

Place names

Use English forms when they are in common use:

> Archangel, Brunswick, Cassel, Castile, Catalonia, Cologne, Cordoba, Corinth, Dagestan, Dnieper, Dniester (but Transnistria), Florence, Genoa, Hanover, Ivory Coast, Lower Saxony, Majorca, Minorca, Munich, Naples, Odessa, Pomerania, Nuremberg, Saxony (and Lower Saxony, Saxony-Anhalt), Sevastopol (not Sebastopol), Seville, Turin.

And English rather than American—Rockefeller Centre, Bar Harbour, Pearl Harbour—unless the place name is part of a company name, such as Rockefeller Center Properties Inc.

Follow local practice when a country expressly changes its name, or the names of rivers, towns, etc, within it. Thus Almaty, not Alma Ata; Balochistan, not Baluchistan; Chennai, not Madras; Chernihiv, not Chernigov; Chur, not Coire; Kolkata, not Calcutta; Kyiv, not Kiev; Lviv, not Lvov; Mumbai, not Bombay; Myanmar, not Burma; Papua, not Irian Jaya; Polokwane, not Pietersburg; Yangon, not Rangoon; and Ulaanbaatar, not Ulan Bator.

But a few exceptions: Ivory Coast, not Côte d'Ivoire; East Timor, not Timor-Leste; and Bangalore, not Bengaluru.

The final s sometimes added by English-speakers to Lyon, Marseille and Tangier now seems precious, so use the s-less form.

In Belgium, use the Dutch or French place name according to which part of the country the place is in.

Tshwane is now the name for the area round Pretoria but not yet for the city itself.

For the Congo that was once called Zaire, Democratic Republic of Congo is fine on first mention, but thereafter, plain Congo (but never the DRC) if there is no risk of confusion with its neighbour. That Congo can be Congo-Brazzaville if necessary. The river is also the Congo. The people of either country are also Congolese.

The Niger delta, like the Mekong, Mississippi and other deltas, is lower case, but the state encompassing part of it is Delta state.

Do not use the definite article before Krajina, Lebanon, Piedmont, Punjab, Sudan, Transkei, Ukraine. But it is the Caucasus, The Gambia, The Hague, the Maghreb, the Netherlands—and La Paz, Le Havre, Los Angeles, etc.

Do not use the names of capital cities as synonyms for their governments. *Britain will send a gunboat* is fine, but *London will send a gunboat* suggests that this will be the action of the people of London alone. To write *Washington and Moscow differ in their approach to Havana* is absurd.

Although the place is *western* (or *eastern*) *Europe*, rhythm dictates that the people are *west* (or *east*) *Europeans*.

Translating foreign names and words

Occasionally, a foreign language may provide the *mot juste*, but use only when it is unusually evocative, hard to translate or in the service of a good joke or pun. Otherwise, find an English alternative.

Foreign names of groups, parties, institutions, etc, should usually be translated: the German *Christian Democratic Union* (not the Christlich Demokratische Union), the *Shining Path* (not Sendero Luminoso), the *National Assembly* (not the Assemblée Nationale). Even some place-names are better translated if they are well known in English: *St Mark's Square* in Venice (not Piazza San Marco), the French *Elysée Palace* (not the Palais de l'Elysée). But if an abbreviation is also given, that may be the initials of the foreign name (so SDP for the *Social Democratic Party of Germany*, PAN for Mexico's *National Action Party*).

Break this rule when the name is better known untranslated: *Parti Québécois*, *Médecins Sans Frontières*. Sometimes this is because the name is hard to translate (eg, *Forza Italia*). If it still seems useful to provide a translation for *Podemos*, etc, the translation should also be in roman, usually in brackets. So *Médecins Sans Frontières* (Doctors Without Borders), *Pravda* (Truth), *zapatero* (shoemaker), etc.

Company names made up of foreign words should be roman: Crédit Agricole, Assicurazioni Generali, etc. Informal names for events, organisations, government programmes, scandals and so on should be set in italics if they are not translated into English: *bracero, ferragosto, harambee, Mitbestimmung, Oportunidades, rentrée, scala mobile, Tangentopoli*, etc. But an English translation will usually be needed, and repeat the foreignism only if it is truly distinctive and hard to translate.

The titles of foreign books, films, plays and operas present difficulties. Some are so well known that they are unlikely to need translation: "Das Kapital", "Mein Kampf", "Le Petit Prince", etc. And sometimes the meaning of the title may be unimportant in the context, so a translation is not necessary: "Hiroshima, Mon Amour". But often the title will be significant, and you will want to translate it. One solution, easy with classics, is to use the English translation alone: "One Hundred Years of Solitude", "The Leopard", "War and Peace", "The Tin Drum", etc. This is usually the best practice to follow with pamphlets, articles and non-fiction, too. But sometimes, especially with books and films lesser known in English (perhaps you are reviewing one), you may want to give both the original title and a translation, thus: "La Règle du Jeu" ("The Rules of the Game"), "La Traviata" ("The Fallen Woman"), etc. Foreign titles do not need to be set in italics.

Accents

On words now accepted as English, use accents (and umlauts) only when they make a crucial difference to pronunciation: *cliché*, *soupçon*, *façade*, *café*, *communiqué*, *exposé*, *über* (but *chateau*, *decor*, *elite*, *feted*, *naive*).

If you use one diacritical mark (except the tilde on the ñ), use all of them: *émigré*, *mêlée*, *protégé*, *résumé*.

Put the accents and other diacritical marks on French, Spanish, Italian, German, Portuguese and Irish names: *François Mitterrand*, *Wolfgang Schäuble*, *Federico Peña*, *José Manuel Barroso*, *Sinn Féin* (though note that some Irish people do not use them; make sure to check whether your subject is a *Sean* or a *Seán*). Leave accents and diacritical marks off other foreign names, unless central to the story (eg, Turkey's efforts to rename itself *Türkiye* in English).

Any foreign word in italics should, however, be given its proper accents.

Naming and other conventions, country by country

Arab words and names

The Arabic alphabet has several consonants which have no exact equivalents in English: for example, two distinct *t*, *d* and *s* sounds, and several consonants pronounced at the back of the mouth and top of the throat. Fastidious transliterators try to reproduce these subtleties with a profusion of apostrophes and *h*s which yield spellings like Mu'ammar al-Qadhdhafi. The risk of error and the ugliness on the page are too great to justify the effort.

Vowels present a lesser problem. There are only three—*a*, *u*, *i*—but each can be lengthened. Do not bother to differentiate between short and long *a*s. Occasionally, a spelling is established where the *u* sound has been lengthened by using *oo*, as in *Sultan Qaboos*. In such instances, follow that convention, but in general go for *ou*, as in *murabitoun* or *Ibn Khaldoun*. For a long *i*-sound the *i* alone will usually do, except in the animate plural ending *-een*, found in *mujahideen*.

Prefer *Muhammad* over *Mohammed*. With Arab names keep the *al-* (lower case) on the first mention of a person's name; this can be dropped on second and subsequent mentions.

All *Abd-* names in Arabic should be hyphenated or be part of a larger word, eg, *Abdallah* or *Abdel-Fattah*. They are all variations of "slave-of" (God, the merciful, the compassionate, etc). None is ever called plain "slave" or "slave of", so better not to have *Abd* or *Abdel/Abdul* stand alone.

Ignore all of the above if a person has a preferred English transliteration; you should use that, eg, *Mohamed ElBaradei*, not *Muhammad al-Baradai*.

The *Al-*, *Al-*, *al* or *al-* (or *Ad-*, *Ar-*, *As-*, etc) before most Arab towns can be dropped (so *Baquba* not *al-Baquba*, *Ramadi* not *ar-Ramadi*). But *al-Quds*, since the fact that it is the Arab name (for Jerusalem) will be important in any context in which it appears.

Some common examples:

Yasser Arafat

Bashar al-Assad (*Mr Assad* on second mention)

Abdel Aziz (founder of kingdom of Saudi Arabia)

Abdel-Fattah al-Sisi

Abdelaziz Bouteflika

Abdullah, King

Abu Mazen (aka Mahmoud
   Abbas)

Abu Musab al-Zarqawi

Abu Nidal

Ahmed Chalabi

Al Saud (when referring to the
   Al Saud as the collectivity
   of the royal house, but
   al-Saud when used as the
   surname of a prince)

Al Thani (without a dash, as
   with Sauds)

Ali al-Sistani (Grand
   Ayatollah)

Anwar Sadat

Aqaba

Barghouti (Marwan &
   Mustafa)

Bashar al-Assad (Mr Assad)

Boutros Boutros-Ghali

burqa

Ennahda, not Nahda

Falluja

Farouq Qaddoumi

Fatah

Gaza Strip (and city)

Habib Bourguiba

Hadith

Hafez Assad

haj

hajj

Hassan, Prince of Jordan

hijab

Hizbullah

Homs

Hosni Mubarak

hudna

Hussein, King

Ibn Khaldoun

Ibrahim al-Jaafari (Dr)

intifada

Jalal Talabani

jamaat islamiya

Jeddah

jihad (but jihadist)

madrasa (in italics)

Majnoon

Marakesh

Maronite

Mohamed ElBaradei

Mosul

Muammar Qaddafi

Muhammad the Prophet

mujahideen (singular,
   mujahid)

Mukhabarat

Muqtada al-Sadr

niqab (in italics)

Nuri al-Maliki

Omar al-Bashir

Qaboos, Sultan

Queen Rania

Peshmerga

Rafik (sic) Hariri

Saddam Hussein

Samarra

Sana'a

Saud al-Faisal, Prince

Saud ibn Abdel Aziz

Seif al-Islam Qaddafi

Shabab (note it is plural)

Sharjah

Sharm el-Sheikh

Shatt al-Arab

169

Strait of Hormuz
Tangier
Tariq Aziz
Wahhabi

Yasser Arafat
Zayed, Sheikh
Zine el-Abidine Ben Ali

Bangladeshi names

Many Bengali speakers do not distinguish between *z* and *j* sounds, and the two letters are often used interchangeably in transliterations into the Latin alphabet. But many Bangladeshi names, in particular, are derived from Arabic, in which the distinction is important. So unless the person is known to prefer another transliteration, for Arabic-derived names, keep the original letter: *Mujibur Rahman* (*Sheikh Mujib* on second reference), *Hefazat, Sajeeb Wajed*.

Belarusian names

If *Belarusians* (not Belarussians) wish to be known by the Belarusian form of their names (*Ihor, Vital*), so be it. But use the familiar, Russian placenames (*Minsk*, not Miensk; *Brest*, not Bryast; *Gomel*, not Homel) and *Alexander Lukashenko*.

Cambodian names

Cambodian names are family name then given name, but on second reference repeat both, adding *Mr* or *Ms*: *Mr Hun Sen, Ms Mu Sochua*.

Chinese names

In general, follow the pinyin spelling of Chinese names, which has replaced older romanisations such as the Wade-Giles system. Peking is therefore *Beijing* and *Mao* is *Zedong*, not *Tse-tung*.

The family name comes first, so *Xi Jinping* becomes *Mr Xi* on second mention.

Some Taiwanese names are still spelt according to Wade-Giles rules; others are spelt idiosyncratically. Other names outside mainland China may also follow Wade-Giles or another romanisation, so make sure to check.

In *Hong Kong*, some people take an English name as well as their Chinese one. The full names of such people should be written with the English name first: *Emily Lau Wai-hing*. On second and subsequent mention, this becomes *Ms Lau*.

Avoid condescending references to the *Middle Kingdom*, a literal translation of China's name for itself, Zhongguo. That name may have more to do with the country's development from a cluster of kingdoms in its centre, rather than an overblown sense of self-importance, and the sobriquet evokes prejudices of another era.

Members of Xinjiang's main non-Han ethnic group are known as *Uyghurs*, without the definite article.

Dutch names

If using first name and surname together, *van* and *den* are lower case: *Dries van Agt* and *Joop den Uyl*. But without their first names they become *Mr Van Agt* and *Mr Den Uyl*. In the case of both a *Van* and a *den*, the *den* is lower-case: *Hans van den Broek* becomes *Mr Van den Broek*. These rules do not always apply to Dutch names in Belgium and South Africa: *Herman Van Rompuy* (thereafter *Mr Van Rompuy*) and *Karel Van Miert* (*Mr Van Miert*).

Ethiopian and Eritrean names

Ethiopians and Eritreans use patronymics, and people are known by their first name followed in most cases by their father's name. Appending a *Mr* or *Ms* to the second name on second reference would have us referring to the person's father. Appending it to the first name would be the equivalent of calling someone "Mr Robert" or "Ms Zanny". We should use first name only on second reference. Thus *Abiy Ahmed* becomes *Abiy* and *Hailemariam Desalegn* becomes *Hailemariam* on second reference.

French names

Any *de* is likely to be lower case, unless it starts a sentence. *De Gaulle* goes up therefore, here; but *Charles de Gaulle* and plain *de Gaulle* go down.

German names

Any *von* is likely to be upper case only at the start of a sentence.

Germany abolished its titles of nobility in 1919, but allowed their holders to continue using them as surnames. Do not imply that someone named *X Graf von Y* is a count. Unusually, these names also change by gender; the female version of *Graf* is *Gräfin* for example.

Icelandic names

Most Icelanders do not have family names. They take their last name (patronymic) from the first name of their father, so *Leifur Eiriksson*, say, is the *son of Eirikur*, and *Freyja Haraldsdottir* is the *daughter of Harald*. If she marries Leifur Eiriksson, she keeps both her names, their son has *Leifsson* as his patronymic and their daughter has *Leifsdottir*. Both names (or more, if someone has two first names) should be used on first mention. On subsequent mentions, use just the first name. A few Icelanders, such as the former prime minister Geir Hilmar Haarde, do have family names, but Icelanders still refer to them only by first name; he is *Geir* on second mention.

Indonesian names

These are generally straightforward, but some Indonesians have only one name. On first mention give it to them unadorned: *Budiono*. Thereafter add the appropriate title: *Mr Budiono*. For those who have several names, be sure to get rid of the correct ones on second and subsequent mentions: *Susilo Bambang Yudhoyono*, for example, was *President* (or *Mr*) *Yudhoyono* on second mention. *Joko Widido* is known as *Jokowi*: note this on first mention and use it without the *Mr* on subsequent mentions.

Italian names

Any *De*, *Della*, *Lo*, etc, is upper case in nearly all names.

In aristocratic names, though, prepositions may refer to an old title (eg, *Visconti di Modrone*, the viscounts of Modrone), where the *di* really is functioning as an *of*, and takes lower case. This is the case even though formal recognition of the titles ended in 1946; the titles are considered a courtesy. So do check.

Japanese names

In accordance with a decree that took effect in 2020, the family name comes first even when written in the Latin alphabet, bringing names in line with how they are said and written in Japanese. So *Kishida Fumio*, not Fumio Kishida, and *Mr Kishida* on second mention.

Khmers Rouges

The followers of various Cambodian communist parties in the 1960s and 1970s were known as *Khmers Rouges*. *Khmer Rouge* may be used as a modifier, but as a standalone noun only to describe a single member of this group.

Korean names

Like many others in the region, Koreans put their family name first.

Note that South Koreans hyphenate their given names: *Kim Dae-jung*. North Koreans have stuck to separate given names, which both take capitals. So *Kim Il Sung*, *Kim Jong Il* and *Kim Jong Un*, etc.

Kyrgyzstan, Kirgiz

Kyrgyzstan is the name of the country. Its adjective is *Kyrgyzstani*, which is also the name of one of its groups of inhabitants. *Kirgiz* is the noun and adjective of the language, and the adjective of *Kirgiz* people outside *Kyrgyzstan*.

Malaysian titles

Tunku, *tengku* or *tuanku*? These are not alternative spellings, but different titles for Malaysian princes which vary according to their state.

Tunku is the title of a prince or princess in the states of Kedah and Negeri Sembilan.

Tengku is used by a prince or princess in Johor, Pahang, Terengganu and Kelantan.

Tuanku is given to a ruler who does not call himself sultan (eg, the rulers of Perlis and Negeri Sembilan), as well as some non-royal nobility in Sarawak.

Myanmar's names and titles

In Myanmar, people take or are given names according to no firm
convention. Names may consist of several words or just one, and
they may be changed more than once during a lifetime. There is no
universal tradition of family names, so each member of a family may
have a name unconnected to any other's. Though some people have
names composed of several words, those parts do not correspond
to the first names and surnames common in other countries. They
may mean *wind* or *gold* or be borrowed from the days of the week. On
second and subsequent mention, therefore, it is usually necessary to
repeat the entire name after the appropriate English title, so *Thein Sein*
(which means *hundreds of thousands of diamonds*) becomes *Mr Thein
Sein*. This practice, however, does not always apply: *Aung San Suu Kyi*
becomes *Ms Suu Kyi*.

A variety of titles are used in Myanmar, of which only *U*, meaning
something close to *Mr*, is likely to be helpful, and then only when
used for well-known figures with one-syllable names such as *U Nu* or
U Thant. Though both these men are dead, to mention either without
the honorific *U* would seem odd. Generally a *U* before a name can be
disregarded. Do not, in particular, refer to *U Anyone*, alive or dead, as
Mr U Anyone: just *U* will do.

Note, however, that an honorific title is occasionally incorporated
into a name, just to make matters even more difficult. And note too
that a *U* at the end of a name is not a title, but usually means *first* or
first-born. Such *U*s are part of the name, so *Thant Myint-U* is always
(*Mr*) *Thant Myint-U*.

Pakistani names

If the name includes the Islamic definite article *ul*, it should be
lower case and without any hyphens: *Zia ul Haq, Mahbub ul Haq* (but
Sadruddin, Mohieddin and *Saladin* are single words).

The genitive *e* is hyphenated: *Jamaat-e-Islami, Muttahida Majlis-e-
Amal*.

Portuguese names

Portuguese surnames are a mirror image of **Spanish** ones (qv): most people have two, but the mother's comes first, then the father's. If they use just one, it is typically the second one, and names are alphabetised under it. *António Luís Santos da Costa* is usually just *António Costa*, and thereafter *Mr Costa*. But some people use both names, especially if their second name is common. That includes *Aníbal Cavaco Silva*, thereafter *Mr Cavaco Silva*. And *Luiz Inácio Lula da Silva* is universally known as *Lula*. Note this on first mention; after that he is *Lula* with no *Mr*.

Roma

Roma is the name of the people. Their language is *Romany*.

Russian words and names

Each approach to transliterating Russian has drawbacks. The following rules aim for phonetic accuracy, except when that conflicts with widely accepted usage.

- No *y* before *e* after consonants: *Belarus, perestroika, Oleg, Lev, Medvedev*. (The actual pronunciation is somewhere between *e* and *ye*.)
- Where pronunciation dictates, put a *y* before the *a* or *e* at the start of a word or after a vowel: *Yavlinsky, Yevgeny* (not Evgeny), *Aliyev* (not Aliev), *Dudayev, Baluyevsky, Dostoyevsky*, etc.
- Words spelled with *ë* in Russian and pronounced *yo* should be spelled *yo*. *Fyodorov* (not Fedorov), *Seleznyov* (not Seleznev), *Pyotr* (not Petr). But stick to *Gorbachev, Khrushchev*, and other famous ones that would otherwise look odd.
- With words that could end *-i, -ii, -y* or *-iy*, use *-y* after consonants and *-i* after vowels. This respects both phonetics and common usage. *Zhirinovsky, Gennady, Yury, Nizhny, Georgy*, etc, but *Bolshoi, Rutskoi, Nikolai, Sergei*. Exception (because conventional): *Tolstoy*.
- Replace *dzh* with *j*. *Jokhar, Jugashvili* (ie, Stalin; but, bowing to convention, give his first name as *Josef*, not Iosif).
- Prefer *Aleksandr, Viktor, Eduard* to Alexander, Victor, Edward,

unless the person involved has clearly chosen an anglicised version. But keep the familiar spelling for historical figures such as *Alexander Nevsky* and *Alexander Solzhenitsyn*.

Sherpa names

The *Sherpa* people are scattered across Nepal, parts of Tibet and a few places in the West, notably New York. If *Sherpa* forms part of a name, it should usually be at the end, not the beginning: *Tenzing Norgay Sherpa*.

Singaporean names

Chinese Singaporean names have no hyphens and the family name comes first: *Lee Hsien Loong*, and thereafter *Mr Lee*.

Spanish names

Spaniards sometimes have several names, usually including two surnames, one from their father and one from their mother, in that order. (In both cases, it is the father's and mother's own father's surname.) Names are alphabetised by the first surname.

Find out which names the person uses publicly. Many people use only the first surname: *Pedro Sánchez Pérez-Castejón* is simply known as *Pedro Sánchez*, and thereafter *Mr Sánchez*.

Often, though, both surnames are used by people whose first surname is common, such as *Fernández, López* or *Rodríguez*. So *Andrés Manuel López Obrador* becomes *Mr López Obrador* and *Juan Fernando López Aguilar* becomes *Mr López Aguilar*. A few people, notably *José Luis Rodríguez Zapatero*, use just the second of their surnames, so he becomes *Mr Zapatero*.

Although on marriage Spanish women sometimes informally add their husband's name (after a *de*) to their own, they do not usually change their legal name.

Swiss place names

Use the familiar English name if there is one (*Chur, Geneva, Lucerne, Zurich*). Otherwise prefer the version used locally (so *Basel* not Basle, *Bern* not Berne.) If a place is officially bilingual, use the name of the larger language group, so *Fribourg* not Freiburg.

Turk, Turkic, Turkmen, Turkoman, etc

Turk, Turkish (noun and adjective of Turkey).

Turkic (adjective applied to one of the branches of the Ural-Altaic family of languages: Uyghur, Kazan Tatar, Kirgiz, etc).

Turkmen (Turkoman or Turkomans living in Turkmenistan; adjective pertaining to them).

Turkmenistani (adjective of Turkmenistan; also a native of that country).

Turkomans (members of a branch of the Turkish peoples mostly living in the region east of the Caspian Sea once known as Turkestan and parts of Iran and Afghanistan; *Turkoman* may also be the language of the Turkmen—and an adjective).

Ukrainian names

Use the official scheme for transliterating Cyrillic to the Roman alphabet filed by the Ukrainian government with the United Nations in 2011, with the following exceptions:

- use a simple *-y* at the end of masculine adjectives that end in Cyrillic ий, ій, ый, including adjective-like names like *Zelensky*.
- no double digraphs (two letters pronounced as one), hence *Zaporizhia* not *Zaporizhzhia*.
- while we have adopted other Ukrainian names such as *Kyiv* and *Kharkiv*, *Odessa* remains thus spelled. The double *s* makes sure the *e* is pronounced correctly.

Vietnamese names

These have no hyphens and the family name comes first:

Ho Chi Minh
Tran Duc Luong (thereafter *Mr Luong*).

9
Confusing cousins: American and British English

The Economist is written in British English. If it is peppered indiscriminately with American terms, many in Britain will find it a *tad* tiresome. Indeed, if we mix national standards, many readers in other countries may be confused at what we are aiming for too.

Many American words and expressions have passed into British English (*movie*); others have vigour (*fracking*, *scofflaw*), or charm (*discombobulate*) or the merit of taking the reader by surprise (*conniptions*). Some are short and to the point (so prefer *lay off* to *make redundant*). But others are unnecessarily long (so use *and* not *additionally*, *car* not *automobile*, *company* not *corporation*, *transport* not *transportation*, *district* not *neighbourhood*, *oblige* not *obligate*, *rocket* not *skyrocket*).

Spat and *scam*, two words beloved by some journalists, have the merit of brevity, but so do *row* and *fraud*; *squabble* and *swindle* might sometimes be used instead. *Normalcy* and *specialty* have good English alternatives, *normality* and *speciality*. *Real estate* is *property*. *Gubernatorial* is an ugly word that can almost always be avoided. Do not *look to* when you mean *hope to* or *intend to*.

Other Americanisms are euphemistic or obscure (so avoid *rookies*, *end runs*, *jury rigs*, *stand-offs*, *point men*, *ball games*, *stepping up to the plate* and almost all other American sporting terms). *Downtown Manhattan* may be a useful term to differentiate it from *uptown* or *midtown Manhattan*, but outside America the adjective to describe the middle of a city is *central*.

And a *judgment call* is a *matter of judgment* or just a *judgment* (if you do not remember the *judgment call of Solomon*, you should prepare for the *last judgment call*). *Fill* forms *in*, not *out*. Use *senior* rather than *ranking*, *rumbustious* rather than *rambunctious*, and *snigger* rather than *snicker*.

In politics, call Washington, DC the *country*'s capital, not the *nation*'s. (And there is no need to use the DC unless there is a risk of confusion with Washington state.) Do not feel obliged to follow American usage in words such as *constituency* (try *supporters*), *perception* (try *belief* or *view*) and *rhetoric* (of which there is too little, not too much—try *language* or *speeches* or *exaggeration* if that is what you mean).

In Britain, though cattle and pigs may be *raised*, children are (or should be) *brought up*.

On-site inspections are allowed, but not *in-flight entertainment*, *on-train teams* or *in-ear headphones*. Throw *stones*, not *rocks*, unless they are of *slate*, which can also mean *abuse* (as a verb) but does not, in Britain, mean *predict*, *schedule* or *nominate*. Do not use *regular* for *ordinary* or *normal*: Mussolini brought in the *regular* train, All-Bran the *regular* man; it is quite *normal* to be without either.

Most *stores* are *shops*. Only the speechless are *dumb*, the well-dressed (and various devices) *smart* and the insane *mad*. *Poster children* should be neither seen nor heard. *Silos* are best kept for grain or, at worst, ballistic missiles. *Scenarios* are for the theatre, *postures* for the gym, *parameters* for the parabola. *Wait* an *hour* or a *month* or a *lifetime*, but not *tables*. Similarly, *grow* a beard or a tomato or even horns, but do not *grow a company* or economy, or *post a profit*.

You may *program* a computer, but in all other contexts the word is *programme*.

British English chooses *one or other thing*; American English chooses *one thing or the other*.

Some American words and expressions were once common in English English (and some are still used in Scottish English). But many now sound old-fashioned to most British ears. So prefer *got* to *gotten*, *doctors* to *physicians*, *lawyers* to *attorneys*, *often* to *oftentimes*, *over* or *too* to *overly*. Wear *clothes* or *clothing* rather than *apparel* or *garments* (or, come to that, *raiment*). Do not *task* people. And never use *likely* to mean *probably*, as in *"He will likely die."*

Prepositions

American and British English often differ in usage of prepositions, prepositional phrases and prepositional verbs. Neither side is consistently more concise. For British English, do not write *meet with* if *meet* alone is clear in the context (ie, that it was not a first meeting). *Outside of* America, *outside* can stand alone. Do not live well *off of* the German welfare system; *off* is enough. But in Britain things go *out of the window*, not just *out the window*.

Nor should you *figure out* if you can *work out*. To *deliver on* a promise means to *keep* it. In British English, doctors and lawyers are to be found *in Harley Street* or *Wall Street*, not *on* it. They rest from their labours *at weekends*, not *on* them. So do children when not *at school* (preferred to *in school*).

When unwell or injured the British go *to hospital* and are then *in hospital* (not *in the hospital*, much less *hospitalised*). British English distinguishes *in future* (ie, *henceforth* or *from now on*, but please not *going forward*) from *in the future* (in the year 2073, say). Americans use *in the future* for both.

Tense

Choose tenses according to British usage, too. In particular, do not *fight shy*—as Americans often do—of the perfect tense, especially where no date or time is given. Thus *Mr Obama has woken up to the danger* is preferable to *Mr Obama woke up to the danger*, unless you can add *last week* or *when he heard the explosion*.

Do not write *Your salary just got smaller so I shrunk the kids*. In British English it is *Your salary has just got smaller so I've shrunk the kids*.

Changes in part of speech

Words jump from one part of speech to another all the time, but different words do so in different directions in British and American English.

Back-formations—like creating the previously nonexistent verb *surveil* from the noun *surveillance*—are common in English. But British and American English differ in which back-formations are accepted. British writers are more likely to use *orientate* for *orient*, while Americans are more likely to use *obligate* for *oblige*. *Curate*, the verb meaning *organise* or *superintend* formed from *curator*, is now acceptable in British English. But it is still too soon for *gallerist* or *galeriste* (prefer *dealer* or, if appropriate, just *gallery*). Please *burgle*, never *burglarise*.

Try not to verb nouns or to adjective them. So do not *action* proposals, *exit* a room, *haemorrhage* red ink, let one event *impact* another, *author* books (still less *co-author* them), *critique* style guides, *pressure* colleagues (*press* will do), *progress* reports, *scope* anything, *showcase* achievements, *source* inputs, *trial* programmes, *loan* money or *gift* anything. To *access* files is (reluctantly) allowed. Avoid *parenting* and, even more assiduously, *parenting skills*.

Instead of *downplaying* criticism, you can *play it down* (or perhaps *make little of it* or *minimise it*). *Upcoming* and *ongoing* are better put as *forthcoming* and *continuing*. Why *outfit* your children when you can *fit* them *out*?

Gunned down means *shot*. And though it is sometimes necessary to use nouns to modify other nouns, there is no need to call an *attempted coup* a *coup attempt*, a *suspected terrorist* a *terrorist suspect* or the *Californian legislature* the *California legislature*. Avoid, too, the habit of throwing together several nouns into one ghastly reticule: *Texas millionaire real-estate developer and failed thrift entrepreneur Hiram Turnipseed...*

Similarly, do not noun adjectives such as *centennial* (prefer *centenary*), *demographic* (usually prefer *demography*), *inaugural* (prefer *inauguration*) and *advisory* (prefer *warning*). Nor should you noun verbs such as *ask* (*request* or *demand*), *assist* (*help*), *build* (*building*), *disconnect* (*disconnection*), *meet* (*meeting*), *spend* (*spending*) and *steer* (*hint* or *guidance*).

Punctuation

commas in lists

The use of a comma before the final *and* in a list is called the serial or Oxford comma: *eggs, bacon, potatoes, and cheese*. Most American writers and publishers use the serial comma; most British writers and publishers use it only when necessary to avoid ambiguity: *eggs, bacon, potatoes and cheese* but *The musicals were by Rodgers and Hammerstein, Sondheim, and Lerner and Loewe.*

full stops (periods)

The American convention is to use full stops (periods) at the end of almost all abbreviations and contractions; specifically, full stops with abbreviations in lower case, a.m., p.m., and no full stops with abbreviations in capitals or small capitals, US, UN, CEO. The British convention is to use full stops after abbreviations—such as *abbr., adj., co.*—but not after *Dr, Mr, Mrs, St.*

hyphens

American English is readier than British English to accept compound words. In particular, many nouns made of two separate nouns are spelt as one word in American English, while in British English they either remain separate or are joined by a hyphen: eg, *applesauce, newborn, commonsense* (hyphenated or two words in British English).

British English also tends, more than American English, to use hyphens as pronunciation aids, to separate repeated vowels in words such as *pre-empt* and *re-examine*, and to join some prefixes to nouns—eg, *pseudo-science*. Americans tend to get rid of hyphens more rapidly than the British, as new editions of dictionaries reflect.

See also Hyphens on pp. 43-4 and 141-2.

quotation marks

In American publications and those of some Commonwealth countries, and also international publications like *The Economist*, the convention is to use double quotation marks, reserving single quotation marks for quotes within quotes. In many British publications (excluding *The Economist*), the convention is the reverse: single quotation marks are used first, then double.

With other punctuation the relative position of quotation marks and other punctuation also differs. The British convention is to place such punctuation according to sense. In general, punctuation goes inside quotation marks when the material quoted is a full sentence. The American convention is simpler but less logical: all commas and full stops precede the final quotation mark, like "this." Other punctuation—colons, semi-colons, question and exclamation marks—is placed according to sense.

See Inverted commas on p. 143 for detailed guidance.

Spelling

Some words are spelt differently in American English and British English. In some cases the American spelling is a survival of 18th-century British usage. In many other cases the differences are due to Noah Webster's reforms of the American spellings, which tended to make American English more obviously phonetic than British English. The word *cosy* becomes *cozy*, *arbour* becomes *arbor*, *theatre* becomes *theater*.

Main spelling differences

-ae/-oe

Although it is now common in British English to write *medieval* rather than *mediaeval*, other words—often scientific terms such as *aeon, diarrhoea, anaesthetic, gynaecology, homoeopathy*—retain their classical composite vowel. In American English, the composite vowel is replaced by a single *e*; thus, *eon, diarrhea, anesthetic, gynecology, homeopathy*. There are exceptions to this in scientific publications. *Fetus* is the preferred spelling on both sides of the Atlantic (not *foetus*).

-ce/-se

In British English, the verb that relates to a noun ending in *-ce* is sometimes given the ending *-se*; thus, *advice* (noun), *advise* (verb), *device/devise, licence/license, practice/practise*. In the first two instances, the spelling change is accompanied by a change in the sound of the word; but in the other two instances, noun and verb are pronounced the same way, and American English spelling reflects this, by using the same spelling for both noun and verb: thus, *license/license* and *practice/practice*. It also extends the use of *-se* to other nouns that in British English are spelt *-ce*: thus, *defense, offense, pretense*.

-e/-ue

The final silent *e* or *ue* of several words is sometimes omitted in American English but retained in British English: thus, *analog/ analogue*, *ax/axe*, *catalog/catalogue*.

-eable/-able

The silent *e*, created when forming some adjectives with this suffix, is more often omitted in American English; thus, *likeable* is spelt *likable*, *unshakeable* is spelt *unshakable*. But the *e* is sometimes retained in American English where it affects the sound of the preceding consonant; thus, *traceable* and *manageable*.

-ize/-ise

The American convention is to spell with *z* many words that some British people and publishers (including *The Economist*) spell with *s*. The *z* spelling is, of course, also a correct British form, used by Oxford University Press (and closer to the Greek from which it comes). Remember, though, that some words must end in *-ise*, whichever spelling convention is being followed. These include:

advertise	despise	incise
advise	devise	merchandise
apprise	disguise	premise
arise	emprise	prise
chastise	enfranchise	revise
circumcise	excise	supervise
comprise	exercise	surmise
compromise	franchise	surprise
demise	improvise	televise

Words with the ending *-lyse* in British English, such as *analyse* and *paralyse*, are spelt *-lyze* in American English.

-ll/-l

In British English, when words ending in the consonant *l* are given a suffix beginning with a vowel (eg, the suffixes *-able*, *-ed*, *-ing*, *-ous*, *-y*), the *l* is doubled; thus, *annul/annulled*, *model/modelling*, *quarrel/ quarrelling*, *rebel/rebellious*, *wool/woolly*. This is inconsistent with the general rule in British English that the final consonant is doubled before the suffix only when the preceding vowel carries the main stress: thus, the word *regret* becomes *regretted*, or *regrettable*; but the word *billet* becomes *billeted*. American English mostly does not have this inconsistency. So if the stress does not fall on the preceding vowel, the *l* is not doubled: thus, *model/modeling*, *travel/traveler*; but *annul/annulled*.

Several words that end in a single *l* in British English—eg, *appal*, *fulfil*—take a double *ll* in American English. In British English the *l* stays single when the word takes a suffix beginning with a consonant (eg, the suffixes *-ful*, *-fully*, *-ment*): thus, *fulfil/fulfilment*. Words ending in *-ll* usually lose one *l* when taking one of these suffixes: thus, *skill/ skilful*, *will/wilfully*. In American English, words ending in *-ll* usually remain intact, whatever the suffix: thus, *skill/skillful*, *will/willfully*.

-m/-mme
American English tends to use the shorter form of ending, thus *gram* and *program*, and British English tends to use the longer: *gramme* and *programme* (but *program* when referring to a computer program, and note that *The Economist* uses *gram* and *kilogram*).

-our/-or
Most British English words ending in *-our*—*ardour*, *behaviour*, *candour*, *demeanour*, *favour*, *valour* and the like—lose the *u* in American English: thus, *ardor*, *candor*, etc. The major exception is *glamour*, which exists alongside *glamor* in American English. (Both types of English lose the *u* in the adjective *glamorous*.) Note, also, that *squalor* is spelt the same on both sides of the Atlantic.

-re/-er
Most British English words ending in *-re*—such as *centre*, *fibre*, *metre*, *theatre*—end in *-er* in American English: thus, *center*, *fiber*, etc. Exceptions include: *acre*, *cadre*, *lucre*, *massacre*, *mediocre*, *ogre*.

-t/-ed
Although this seems to be a mere difference in spelling the past tense of some verbs, it can also represent a different form with a different meaning. Both forms of ending are acceptable in British English,

but the -*t* form is dominant—*burnt, learnt, spelt*—whereas American English uses -*ed*: *burned, learned, spelled*. Contrarily, British English uses -*ed* for the past tense and past participle of certain verbs—*quitted, sweated*—while American English can use the infinitive spelling—*quit, sweat*. Some verbs have a different form of past tense and past participle, eg, the past tense of *dive* is *dived* in British English but *dove* in American English, and the past tense of *fit* is always *fit* in American English, not *fitted*, as in British English.

Common spelling differences

American	British
American	**British**
aging	ageing
aluminum	aluminium
apothegm	apophthegm
behoove	behove
check	cheque
checkered (pattern)	chequered
cozy	cosy
draft	draught
dike	dyke
furor	furore
gray	grey
jeweler/jewelry	jeweller/jewellery
curb/curbside	kerb/kerbside
licorice	liquorice
maneuver/maneuverable	manoeuvre/manoeuvrable
mold/molder/molt	mould/moulder/moult
mustache	moustache
plow	plough
pudgy	podgy
rambunctious	rumbustious
skeptic	sceptic
specialty store	specialist shop
specialty	speciality (but specialty medicine, steel, chemicals)

sulfur	sulphur (but sulfur in scientific publications)
tidbit	titbit
toward	towards
tire	tyre
vise	vice (tool)

Dates

Americans are at odds with the rest of the world in the way they express dates in numerical form. In Britain and elsewhere, the order is always day, month, year—eg, 7/9/2020 for September 7th 2020. In the United States, it is month, day, year—eg, 9/7/2020. This can lead to misunderstanding, not least with the common term "9/11" to refer to the destruction of the World Trade Centre on September 11th 2001, which the rest of the world will automatically translate as November 9th.

Education

Children in school are *pupils* in British English, not *students*. When they *leave* (or, in America, *graduate*), they go to *college* or *university*, not *school*. Remember, too, that in America *tuition* is often used for *tuition fees*. In *The Economist*, however, if *tuition* increases, that should mean *instruction* increases, not *the bill* for it. And in Britain, *public schools* are the places where fee-paying parents send their children; in the United States, they are places where they don't. (*Private school* is also increasingly used in Britain for schools that charge fees. But do not use the euphemism *independent schools*.)

Cultural references

What is familiar in one culture may be entirely alien in another. British English exploits terms and phrases borrowed from the game of cricket; American English uses baseball terms. Those writing for readers in both markets use either set of terms at their peril. Do not make references or assumptions that are geographically exclusive, for example by specifying months or seasons when referring to seasonal patterns, or by using north or south to imply a type of climate.

Units of measurement

In British publications measurements are now largely expressed in SI units (the modern form of metric units), although imperial measures are still used in certain contexts. In American publications measurements may be expressed in SI units, but imperial units are still more common.

Although the British imperial and American standard measures are usually identical, there are some important exceptions, eg, the number of fluid ounces in a pint: 16 in the American system and 20 in the British. This difference has a knock-on effect in the volumes of gallons, which are smaller in America than in Britain. Americans also use the measure *quart* (one-quarter of a gallon), which is now considered archaic in Britain.

American-to-British glossary

The following lists draw attention to commonly used words and idioms that are spelt differently or have different meanings in American English and British English.

American	British
additional paid-in capital	share premium
allowances	provisions
amortisation	depreciation
antenna	aerial (tv)
apartment	flat
appetizer	starter
arugula	rocket (salad)
attorney	lawyer
attorney, lawyer	solicitor
auto-racing	motor-racing
baby carriage, stroller	pram, push-chair
bathrobe/housecoat/robe	dressing gown

bathroom, restroom	lavatory, toilet
beltway	ring road
bill	banknote
bobby pins	hairgrips
braid	plait
broil (verb), broiler (noun)	grill (verb and noun)
bus	coach
bylaws	articles of association
calendar	diary (appointments)
call collect	reverse charges
call, phone	phone
candied	crystallised
candy	sweets
capital leases	finance leases
cell phone	mobile phone
Certified Public Accountant (CPA)	Chartered Accountant (CA)
check (restaurant)	bill
checking account	current account
cilantro (the leafy bit)	coriander
closet	clothes cupboard/wardrobe
common stock	ordinary shares
cookie	biscuit (sweet)
coriander (the spice)	ground coriander
corn	maize/sweetcorn
corn syrup	golden syrup
cornstarch	cornflour
cot	camp bed
counterclockwise	anti-clockwise
cracker	biscuit (savoury)
crawfish	crayfish
crib	cot
crosswalk	pedestrian crossing
current rate method	closing rate method
Daylight Saving Time	British Summer Time (BST)

deferred income tax	deferred tax
defogger	demister
diaper	nappy
divided highway	dual carriageway
driver's license	driving licence
drugstore, pharmacy	chemist
dumb	stupid
eggplant	aubergine
electrical outlet, socket	power point
elevator	lift
entrée	main course
exhibit	exhibition (unless a single item)
extract or flavoring	essence (eg, vanilla)
fall	autumn
fender	bumper
figure out	work out (problem)
first floor	ground floor
flashlight	torch
flat tire	puncture
flour, all-purpose	flour, plain
flour, self-rising	flour, self-raising
flour, whole-wheat	flour, wholemeal
French fries	chips
fruit and vegetable store	greengrocer's
garbage can, trash can	dustbin
gas pedal	accelerator
gas/service station	petrol station
gasoline, gas	petrol
golden raisin	sultana
goose-bumps	goose-pimples
gotten	got (past participle)
ground	earthed (wire)
ground meat	minced meat
hamburger meat, ground beef	mince
heavy cream	double cream

highway, freeway, expressway	motorway
home away from home	home from home
homely	plain-looking, unattractive
homey	homely
hood (car)	bonnet
horseback riding	riding
housing development	housing estate
Internal Revenue Service	HM Revenue and Customs
intersection	crossroads/junction
journal	diary (record)
jumper cables	jump leads
lease on life	lease of life
license plate	number plate
light cream	single cream
line (noun), line up	queue (noun and verb)
mail, mailbox	post, post box
main street	high street
mean	nasty, cruel
molasses	black treacle
movie	film
movie theater	cinema
muffler (car)	exhaust
nominate a candidate	adopt a candidate
obligate	oblige
one-way ticket	single ticket
ouster	ousting
outage	power cut
overly (as in too much)	over
overpass	flyover
pacifier (baby's)	dummy
pants, slacks, trousers	trousers
pantyhose, (opaque) tights	tights
par value	nominal value
parking lot	car park
pavement	road surface

pedestrian underpass	subway
physician	doctor
pie crust	pastry case
pitted (cherries, etc)	stoned
plaid	tartan
plastic wrap	cling film
platform (political)	manifesto
(potato) chips	crisps
potholder	oven glove
powdered or confectioners' sugar	icing sugar
preferred stock	preference shares
price hike	price rise
principal	headmistress/headmaster
private school	public school
public housing, housing project	council estate
public school	state school
purchase accounting	acquisition accounting
purse, pocketbook	handbag, wallet
rain-check	postponement
raise	pay rise
ramp	slip road
ranking (politician)	senior
real estate	property
realtor/real estate agent	estate agent
regular, normal	ordinary
rent (a car, etc)	hire
restricted surplus or deficiency	undistributable reserves
revenues	turnover
rider	passenger
round-trip ticket	return ticket
row house	terraced house
rowboat	rowing boat
run (in stocking)	ladder
run for office	stand for office

sailboat	sailing boat
sawed-off shotgun	sawn-off shotgun
savings and loan association	building society
scallion, green onion	spring onion
seeds (in fruit)	pips
senior citizen, senior	old-age pensioner, OAP
short pastry/basic pie dough	shortcrust pastry
sidewalk	pavement
smart (non-tech sense)	clever, shrewd, astute
snaps	press studs
Social Security	old-age pension, state pension
somewhat (*quite* means *very*)	quite
soy	soya
sport jacket	sports jacket
station wagon	estate car
stingy, tight	mean
stock dividend or stock split	bonus or scrip issue
stockholders' equity	shareholders' funds
story, floor	storey
subway	underground (or tube train, metro)
suspenders	braces
sweet pepper, bell pepper, capsicum	pepper (red, green, etc)
teller	clerk (bank)
trailer, motorhome, RV	caravan
train station	railway station
transmission	gearbox
transportation	transport
Treasury stock	Treasury share
trial lawyer	barrister
truck	lorry
trunk	boot, car
turn signal	indicator
turnoff	turning (road)

two weeks	fortnight
underpants	pants
(sleeveless) undershirt	vest
unusual items	exceptional items
upscale	upmarket
vacation	holiday
vest	waistcoat
veteran	ex-serviceman
wading pool	paddling pool
walker	Zimmer frame
washcloth	flannel
windshield	windscreen
wrench	spanner
yield	give way
zee (the letter)	zed
zip code	post code
zipper	zip (noun)
zucchini	courgette

Particular problems

Several terms and expressions may cause confusion and are therefore best avoided, or at least used with care and perhaps explained. They include:

constituency

In Britain this was long used to mean either a *body of voters who elect a representative to a legislature* or the *place thus represented*. In the United States *constituency* is used differently, to mean an *interest-group* or *component of a power-base*. What the British call a *constituency*, Americans call a *district*, Canadians a *riding* and Australians an *electorate*. In *The Economist* try to use *constituency* only in its long-standing British sense and in all contexts make the meaning clear, if necessary by writing *electoral district*.

federalist
In Britain, in the context of the EU, someone who believes in centralising the powers of associated states; in the United States (and Germany), someone who believes in decentralising them.

liberal
In Europe, someone who believes above all in the freedom of the individual; in the United States, someone who believes in the progressive tradition of Franklin Roosevelt. Increasingly in America, those furthest to the left call themselves progressives. In any case, make sure the context makes clear what you mean, and anywhere outside America, reserve liberal for its "freedom of the individual" sense.

moot (qv, Chapter 6)
In British English, this means *arguable*, *doubtful* or *open to debate*; in the United States, it means *hypothetical* or *academic*, ie, *of no practical significance*.

offensive
In Britain, *offensive* (as an adjective) usually means *rude*. In America, it can also mean *attacking*, as in *offensive weapons*. Similarly, to the British an *offence* is usually a crime or *transgression*. For Americans, especially in sport, *offense* is the opposite of *defense*.

quite
In America, *quite* is an intensifying adverb similar to *altogether*, *entirely* or *very*; in Britain, depending on the emphasis, the tone of voice and the adjective that follows, it usually means *fairly*, *moderately* or *reasonably* and will often not be taken as a compliment if it modifies one.

red and blue
In Britain, colours that are associated with socialism and Conservatism respectively; in the United States, colours that are associated with Republicans and Democrats respectively. *Red states* and *blue states* (districts, etc) are firmly established in American discourse now, but try to make clear on first mention what these are for readers unfamiliar with them.

Social Security
In America, *Social Security* means *pensions*; elsewhere it usually means *state benefits* more generally, which are called *welfare* in the United States.

table
In Britain, the act of bringing something forward for action; in the United States, just the opposite.

torrid
This is used in both countries to mean *scorching*, and by extension *intense*, as in a *torrid affair*. But *torrid* is used in American journalese to mean a *hot period*, in a good way: a baseball player who has hit four home runs in four consecutive games is on a *torrid streak*. In contrast, *torrid times* are full of problems in Britain.

transportation
In the United States, a means of getting from A to B; in Britain, a means of getting rid of convicts.

10
Reference

Upper and lower case

upper case (miscellaneous)

Anglophone (but prefer
   English-speaking)
Antichrist
anti-Semitism
Atlanticist
the Bar
the Belt and Road Initiative
   (BRI)
Berlin Wall
the Bible (but biblical)
Bill of Rights
Bunds (the German bonds)
Catholics (but Roman
   Catholic church on first
   mention)
Chapter 8 (etc)
Christ
Christmas Day
Christmas Eve
Coloureds (in South Africa)
Cubism (-ist)
the Cup Final
Dalit (etc)
the Davis Cup
D-Day

Earth (when, and only when,
   it is being discussed as a
   planet like Mars or Venus)
Eurobond
Euroyen bond
Fauvism (-ist)
Fifth Republic (France)
First Lady
Founding Fathers
Francophone (but prefer
   French-speaking)
General Assembly (UN)
Hispanics
House of Laity
Impressionist
Iron Curtain
the King's/Queen's Speech
Koran
Labour Day
Lava Jato
Mafia (the genuine article
   only)
Marine Corps
   (but marines)
May Day

Mecca (in Saudi Arabia,
　California and Liberia)
Memorial Day
Modernism (-ist)
Moon (when Earth's moon)
　(but sun)
National Guard (US)
New Year's Eve
North Pole
Orthodox (Jews, Christians)
Pershing missile
Protestants

Revolutionary Guard(s) (in,
　eg, Iran)
Russify
Semitic (-ism)
Stealth fighter, bomber
Taser
Ten Commandments
Test match
Tube (London Underground)
Utopia (for the book and the
　place in it, but lower case
　when generic)
Wild West

lower case (miscellaneous)

administration
amazon (female warrior)
angst
Arab spring
balkanised
blacks
byzantine (unless you mean
　the empire)
cabinet
Christian democratic (if not
　referring to a party of that
　name)
civil servant
civil service
civil war (even America's)
cold war
common market
communist (generally)
constitution (even America's)
cruise missile
draconian
euro (the currency)

electoral college
first world war
french windows, fries
general synod
gentile
government
Gulf war
gypsy (as a generic, but Roma
　for the ethnic group)
heaven (and hell)
internet
junior (as in Douglas
　Fairbanks junior)
Kyoto protocol
the left
loyalist
mafia (any old group of
　criminals)
mecca (as in Jermyn Street is
　a mecca for lovers of loud
　shirts)
northern lights

Olympic games (and Asian,
Commonwealth, European,
etc). But Winter Olympics
opposition
parliament (meaning
the term during which
Parliament sits)
philistine
platonic
the pope
the press
pyrrhic
the queen
quisling
realpolitik
republican (unless referring
to a party of that name)
revolution (everyone's, but
qualifier up, as in Green,

Orange, Jasmine, etc.)
the right
second world war
self-defence forces (Japan)
senior (as in Douglas
Fairbanks senior)
the shah
state-of-the-union message
the sunbelt
third world
titanic, titans (unless the
original Titans)
utopia, utopian (generic)
war of independence
war of 1812
white paper
world wide web
young turk

Hyphenated and compound nouns

titles

vice-president
director-general
under-secretary
secretary-general
attorney-general
solicitor-general

but
general secretary
deputy secretary
deputy director
district attorney

miscellaneous words

If you cannot find your word(s) here, consult the Chambers dictionary.

one word

3D
airfield
airspace

airtime
antibiotic
anticlimax

antidote
antiseptic
antitrust
backlash
backyard
banknote
barcode
bedfellow
bestseller (-ing)
bilingual
blackboard
blacklist, whitelist
blackout
blueprint
bookmaker
boomtown
brasshat
businessman
bypass
carjacking
carmaker
carpetbagger
cashflow
catchphrase
ceasefire
checklist
chipmaker
clampdown
clockmaker
cloudcuckooland
coalminer
coastguard
codebreaker
comeback
commonsense (adj)
crossfire
cryptocurrency
cyberspace

dealmaking
decommission
deepwater (adj)
diehard
dotcom
downturn
fallout
farmworker
faultline
figleaf
flipside
foothold
forever (adverb, when it
    precedes the verb)
foxhunter (-ing)
freshwater (adj)
fundraiser (-ing)
gasfield
gatekeeper
goodwill
grassroots (adj and noun)
groupspeak, etc
halfhearted
halfway (adj or adv)
handout
handpicked
handwriting
hardline
hardworking
headache
hijack
hobnob
housebuilding
infrared
ironclad
jobhunter
keyword
knockout

kowtow
lacklustre
lamppost
landmine
landowner
laptop
lockout
logjam
longtime
loophole
lopsided
lukewarm
machinegun
marketmaker (-ing)
metalworker
midterms
minefield
multilingual
nationwide (try national)
nevertheless
newsweekly
nitpicker (-ing)
nonetheless
offline
offshore
oilfield
oneupmanship
online
onshore
orangutan
outsource
overpaid
overrated
overreach
override
overrule
overrun
payout

paywall
peacekeepers (-ing)
peacemaker (-ing)
peacetime
petrochemical, petrodollars
phrasebook
pickup truck
piggyback
placeholder
policymakers (-ing), but
    foreign-policy makers
    (-ing)
prizewinner, prizewinning
profitmaking
proofread (-er, -ing)
rainforest
reopen
ringtone
roadblock
rulebook
rundown
rustbelt
safekeeping
salesforce
saltwater (adj)
seabed
seawater (adj)
scaremonger,
    scaremongering
shantytown
shipbroker (-ing)
shipbuilder (-ing)
shipowner
shortcut
shorthand
shortlist
shutdown
sidestep

skyscraper
smartphone, smartcard, etc
socioeconomic
soulmate
soyabean
spillover
startup
statewide
steamroll, steamrolled
steelmaker (-ing)
steelworker (-ing)
stillborn
stockmarket
streetlight
streetwalker
strongman
subcommittee
subcontinent
subcontract
subhuman
submachinegun
subprime
sunbelt
superdelegates (US)
superpower
takeover
textbooks
threshold

timetable
toolkit
touchscreen
trademark
transatlantic
transpacific
troublemaker (-ing)
turnout
ultraviolet
underdog
underpaid
underrated
upfront
videodisc
videocassette
wartime
watchdog
website
whistleblower
wildflower (adj, but noun
   wild flowers)
windfall
workforce
worldview
worldwide (but world wide
   web)
worthwhile
wrongdoing

two words

3D printer
ad hoc (always)
aid worker
air base
air strike
air force
all right
any time

any more
arm's length
asset recycling
ballot box
birth rate
blind spot
body count
body politic

call centre
career woman
child care (noun)
cluster bombs
common sense
   (noun)
computer
   scientist

dare say
data set
errand boy
flood plain
foot soldier
for ever (after a
    verb)
free fall
fresh water
    (noun)
front line (noun)
health care
hedge fund
home page
home town

joint venture
Land Rover
life raft
Nobel
    prizewinner
no one
pay cheque
photo
    opportunity
playing field
plea bargain
resting place
road map
road works
salt water (noun)

sat nav
sea water (noun)
soap opera
some day
some time
sugar cane
supply chain,
    line, etc
truck driver
under way
vice versa
wild flowers
    (but adj,
    wildflower)

hyphenated (two elements)

agri-business
air-conditioning
    (do not use
    A/C)
aircraft-carrier
air-miles
air-traffic control
anti-retroviral
asylum-seekers
baby-boomer
back-story
back-up
bail-out (noun)
balance-sheet
basket-case
bell-ringer
brand-new
break-even
break-up (noun)
breast-feed

build-up (noun)
bumper-sticker
buy-out (noun)
call-up (noun)
clearing-house
climb-down
come-uppance
copper-miner
counter-attack,
    -intuitive, etc
court-martial
    (noun and
    verb)
cover-up
crowd-funding
current-account
    deficit
death-squads
derring-do
down-payment

drawing-board
drug-dealer (-ing)
drug-trafficker
    (-ing)
drunk- (not
    drink) driving
end-game
end-year
extra-territorial,
    extra-
    territoriality
faint-hearted
far-sighted
field-worker
film-maker
foot-soldiers or
    footsoldiers
fore-runner
fortune-teller
front-line (adj)

front-runner
fund-raiser
get-together
(noun)
grand-daughter
grown-up
guide-dog
gun-owner
gun-runner
hand-held
have-not (noun)
heir-apparent
high-rise (noun)
hit-list
home-made
hostage-taker
hot-head
hydro-electric
ice-cream
ill-health
ill-tempered
in-fighting
inter-ethic, inter-
governmental
interest-group
kerb-crawler
know-how
laid-back
land-grab
laughing-stock
launch-pad
lay-off (noun)
like-minded
line-up
long-standing
long-term (adj)
machine-tool
m-health

mid-term, mid-
way, mid-week,
mid-August,
etc
mill-owner
money-
laundering
member-states
narrow-bodied
nation-building
nation-state
nest-egg
new-found
newly-wed
news-stand
night-time
Nobel-
prizewinning
non-violent
non-partisan
number-plate
on-side
over-expansion
over-riding
pay-off (noun)
pipe-dream
place-name
plain-clothes (NB
not clothed)
point-man
post-modern,
post-war
pot-hole
power-struggle
pow-wow
power-broker
press-gang
pressure-group

pre-nup
pre-school (but
prefer nursery)
pre-war
print-out
pull-out (noun,
not verb)
question-mark
rain-check
re-create, -tion
(meaning
create again)
re-present
(meaning
present again)
re-sent (meaning
sent again)
re-sort (meaning
sort again)
re-treat (meaning
treat again)
re-run
re-use
ring-fence
round-up (noun)
running-mate
run-off, run-up
safety-net,
safety-valve
sea-change
search-and-
rescue
second-hand
set-up (noun)
shake-out (noun)
shoot-out
short-sighted
side-effect

slum-dweller
sound-bite
stand-off (noun)
starting-point
sticking-point
stop-gap
stumbling-block
subject-matter
sub-Saharan
suicide-bomb
 (-er, -ing)
swan-song
talking-shop
take-off

task-force
tear-gas
tech-speak
think-tank
time-bomb
trade-off (noun)
truck-driver
turning-point
ultra-nationalist
under-age
under-used
voice-mail
voice-over
vote-rigging

vote-winner
war-chest
well-being
well-placed
wide-bodied
Wi-Fi
Wi-Max
wind-down
 (noun)
window-dressing
wish-list
witch-hunt
working-party

three words

ad hoc agreement (meeting,
 etc)
chief(s) of staff
consumer price index
Ease of Doing Business Index
 (World Bank)
Federal Open Market
 Committee
level playing field
half a dozen
in as much
in so far

national security adviser
nuclear power station
randomised controlled trial
 (not control trial)
sovereign wealth fund
third world war (if things get
 bad)
world wide web
year on year (when not
 modifying noun as in year-
 on-year growth)

three hyphenated words

A-turned-B (unless this leads
 to something unwieldy,
 eg, jobbing churchwarden
 turned captain of industry)
brother-in-law
chock-a-block
commander-in-chief

multiple-rocket-launcher
no-man's-land
prisoners-of-war
second-in-command
stock-in-trade
track-and-field

three or four words, two hyphenated
　armoured personnel-carrier
　troubled asset-relief programme

years, dates
Do not write *from 1947-50* (write *in 1947-50* or *from 1947 to 1950*) and *between 1961-65* (write *in 1961-65, between 1961 and 1965* or *from 1961 to 1965*).

Italics, roman type, in quotation marks, etc

foreign words and phrases
Should be set in italics:

ancien régime	*in camera*	*perestroika*
cabinet (French	*intifada*	*sarariman*
type)	*loya jirga*	*Schadenfreude*
de rigueur	*mani pulite*	*trahison des clercs*
fatwa	*Mitbestimmung*	*ujamaa*
glasnost	*pace*	
Hindutva	*papabile*	

Unless they are so familiar that they have become anglicised, when they should be in roman:

ad hoc	de facto, de jure
apartheid	elite
a priori	en masse, en route
a propos	halal
avant-garde	in situ
bête noire	jihad
bona fide	kosher
bourgeois	machismo
café	nouveau riche
chargé d'affaires	persona non grata
coup d'état (but *coup de*	parvenu
foudre, coup de grâce,	pogrom
etc)	post mortem

putsch	tabula rasa
raison d'être	tsunami
realpolitik	vice versa
sharia	vis-à-vis
status quo	

Remember to put appropriate accents and diacritical marks on all foreign words in italics (and give initial capital letters to German nouns when in italics, but not if not). Make sure that the meaning of any foreign word you use is clear. Foreign language quotations are in quotes and roman. For the scientific names of animals, plants, etc. see Latin names, p. 114.

newspapers, periodicals, television and works of art

The Economist has *The* italicised. But this is an exception, thus the *Daily Telegraph*, the *New York Times*, the *Observer* (but *Le Monde*, *Die Welt*, *Die Zeit*). The *Yomiuri Shimbun* should be italicised, but you can also say the *Yomiuri*, or the *Yomiuri* newspaper, since *shimbun* simply means newspaper in Japanese. But the *Nikkei*, an abbreviation (for *Nihon Keizai*), should not be written as *Nikkei Shimbun*, as that is not strictly this financial daily's name. *People's Daily* needs no *the*.

Books, films, pamphlets, plays, radio programmes, operas, video games and television programmes are roman, with capital letters for each main word, in quotation marks. Thus: "Pride and Prejudice", "Much Ado about Nothing", "La Traviata", "Any Questions", "Crossfire", etc. The same rules apply to *Symphonies* and *Masses*: "Mozart's Symphony in G Minor". But *the Bible* and its books (Genesis, Ecclesiastes, John, etc) take no inverted commas.

Online news publications and *magazines* take italics and lower case *the*. *Blogs* are roman.

Computer games are in quote marks: "Angry Birds"; *all other apps* are without: Instagram, Whatsapp.

lawsuits

Thus: *Brown v Board of Education*, *Jarndyce v Jarndyce* (in italics). If abbreviated, *versus* should always be shortened to *v*, with no point after it.

Plurals

-a

consortia	memoranda	sanatoria
corrigenda	millennia	spectra
data	phenomena	strata
media	quanta	

-ae

alumnae	amoebae
antennae	formulae

-eaus

bureaus	plateaus

-eaux

chateaux	tableaux

-fs, -efs

dwarfs	roofs
oafs	still-lifes

-i

alumni	termini	stimuli
nuclei	bacilli	

-oes

archipelagoes	haloes	potatoes
buffaloes	heroes	salvoes
cargoes	innuendoes	tomatoes
desperadoes	mangoes	tornadoes
dominoes	mementoes	torpedoes
echoes	mosquitoes	vetoes
embargoes	mottoes	volcanoes
frescoes	noes	

-os

albinos	flamingos	placebos
armadillos	folios	provisos
calicos	ghettos	quangos
casinos	impresarios	radios
commandos	librettos	silos
demos	manifestos	solos
dynamos	memos	sopranos
egos	mulattos	stilettos
embryos	neutrinos	virtuosos
falsettos	oratorios	weirdos
fandangos	peccadillos	zeros
fiascos	pianos	

-s

agendas

-ums

conundrums	moratoriums	stadiums
crematoriums	nostrums	symposiums
curriculums	premiums	ultimatums
emporiums	quorums	
forums	referendums	

-uses

buses	fetuses	prospectuses
caucuses	focuses	syllabuses
circuses	geniuses	

-ves

calves	loaves	wharves
halves	scarves	
hooves	turves	

Note: *indexes* (of books), but *indices* (indicators, index numbers); *attorneys-general, secretaries-general, solicitors-general*, etc; but *lord lieutenants*, not *lords lieutenant* (they are not lords).

Common spelling problems

abattoir
abut, abutted, abutting
accommodate
acknowledgment
acquittal, acquitted, acquitting
adrenalin
adviser, advisory
aeon
aeroplane, aircraft, airliner
aesthetic
aficionado
Afrikaans (the language), Afrikaner (the person)
ageing (but caging, imaging, paging, raging, waging)
agri-business (not agro-business)
algorithm
al-Qaeda
amiable
amid (not amidst)
amok (not amuck)
analogue (not analog)
annex (verb), annexe (noun)
antecedent
appal, appals, appalling, appalled
aqueduct
aquifer
arbitrager
arraign
artefact
asinine
balk (not baulk)
balloted, balloting

bandanna
bandwagon
barrelled
battalion
bellwether
benefiting, benefited
biased
bicentenary (noun, not bicentennial)
billeting, billeted
blanketing, blanketed
bloc (for a set of countries, etc)
blowzy (not blousy)
bogey (bogie is on a locomotive)
borsch
braggadocio
brethren
bumf
bused, busing (keep bussing for kissing)
by-election, bypass, by-product, bylaw, byword
bye (in sport)
caesium
caddie (golf), caddy (tea)
cancelling, cancelled
cannon (gun), canon (standard, criterion, clergyman, oeuvre)
cappuccino
carcass
caviar
chameleon
chancy

channelling, channelled

checking account (spell it
thus when explaining
to Americans a current
account, which is to be
preferred)

choosy

Church of Jesus Christ of
Latter-day Saints

cipher

clubable (coined, and
spelled thus, by Dr
Johnson)

colour, colouring, colourist

combating, combated

commemorate

confectionery

connection

consensus

cooled, cooler, coolly

coral (stuff found in sea),
corral (cattle pen)

coruscate

cosseted, cosseting

curtsy (not curtsey)

debacle

defendant

dependant (person),
dependent (adj)

depository (unless referring
to American depositary
receipts)

de rigueur

desiccate, desiccation

detente (not détente)

Deutschmark, D-mark

dexterous (not dextrous)

diarrhoea

dignitary

dilapidate

dispatch (not despatch)

dispel, dispelling

distil, distiller

divergences

doppelganger(s)

doveish

dry, dryer, driest (adjectives)

dryer (for clothes, hair)

dryly

dullness

dwelt

dyeing (colour)

dyke

ecstasy

embarrass (but harass)

encyclopedia

enroll, enrolment

ensure (make certain), insure
(against risks)

enthrall

extrovert

faeces, faecal, but defecate

farther (distance), further
(additional)

favour, favourable

ferreted

fetus (not foetus)

field-marshal

Filipino, Filipina (person),
Philippine (adj of the
Philippines)

filleting, filleted

flotation

flyer, frequent flyer, high-
flyer

focused, focusing

forbear (abstain), forebear
(ancestor)
forbid, forbade
foreboding
foreclose
forefather
forestall
forewarn
forgather
forgo (do without), forego
(precede)
forsake
forswear, forsworn
freelance (not freelancer)
fuelled, fuelling, refuelling
-ful, not -full (thus armful,
bathful, handful, etc)
fulfil, fulfilling
fullness
fulsome
funnelling, funnelled
furore
gallivant
gelatine
gist (not jist)
glamour, glamorise,
glamorous
graffito, graffiti
gram (not gramme)
grey
guerrilla
gulag
gypsy
haj
hajj
harass (but embarrass)
hiccup (not hiccough)
high-tech

highfalutin
Hizbullah
honour, honourable
hotch-potch (not hodge-
podge)
humour, humorist,
humorous
hurrah (not hooray)
idiosyncrasy
impostor
impresario
inadvertent
incur, incurring
innocuous
inoculate
inquire, inquiry (not enquire,
enquiry)
install, instalment,
installation
instil, instilling
Inter Services Intelligence
agency (ISI)
intransigent
jail (not gaol)
jewellery (not jewelry)
jihad, jihadist
judgment
kibosh
kilogram or kilo (not
kilogramme)
"Kum Bay Yah"
labelling, labelled
laissez-faire
lambast (not lambaste)
launderette
leaned (not leant)
leukaemia
levelled

libelling, libelled
licence (noun), license (verb),
　licensee (person with a
　licence)
limited
linchpin, lynch law
liquefy
literal
logarithm
littoral (shore)
loth (reluctant), loathe (hate),
　loathsome
low-tech
manilla envelope, but Manila,
　capital of the Philippines
manoeuvre, manoeuvring
marshal (noun and verb),
　marshalled
mayonnaise
Médecins Sans Frontières
medieval
mêlée
memento
mileage
millennium, but millenarian
mimicked, mimicking
minuscule
moccasin
modelling, modelled
monied (not moneyed)
mould
mujahideen
Muslim (not Moslem)
naivety
'Ndrangheta
nimbyism
nine-dash line
nonplussed

North-east passage
nosy
nought (for numerals),
　otherwise naught
obbligato
occur, occurring
oenology
oesophagus
oestrus (oestrogen, etc)
ophthalmic (ophthalmology,
　etc)
optics (optician, etc)
orangutan
outsize (not outsized)
paediatric, paediatrician
palaeontology,
　palaeontologist
panel, panelled
paraffin
parallel, paralleled
Parti (and Bloc) Québécois
Pashto (language), Pashtun
　(people)
pastime
pavilion
pedlar (not peddler)
phoney (not phony)
phosphorus
piggyback (not pickaback)
plummeted, plummeting
poky
Politburo
practice (noun), practise
　(verb)
praesidium (not presidium)
predilection
preferred (preferring, but
　proffered)

preternatural (not praeternatural)

preventive (not preventative)

primeval

pricey

principal (head, loan; or adj), principle (abstract noun)

proffered (proffering, but preferred)

profited

program (only in a computer context, incl. online teaching programs); otherwise programme

prophecy (noun)

prophesy (verb)

protester

pukka

Pulitzer

pygmy

pyrrhic

pzazz

Queensberry (Marquess of and so eponymous rule-maker)

queuing

rack, racked, racking (as in racked with pain, nerve-racking)

racket

rankle

rarefy

razzmatazz

recur, recurrent, recurring

Red Army Fraction (not Faction)

regretted, regretting

restaurateur

resuscitate

rhythm

rivet (riveted, riveter, riveting)

rococo

ropy

rouble (not ruble)

rumbustious

rumoured

sacrilegious

sanatorium

sarariman

savannah

Schadenfreude

seize

shaky

sharia (not Sharia law)

sheriff

shenanigans

Shia (noun and adj), Shias, Shiism

shibboleth

shoo-in

Sibylline

siege

sieve

siphon (not syphon)

skulduggery

smelt (not smelled)

smidgen (not smidgeon)

smoky

smooth (both noun and verb)

snigger (not snicker)

sobriquet

somersault

soothe

souped up

soyabean
specialty (only in context
    of medicine, steel and
    chemicals), otherwise
    speciality
sphinx
spoilt
squirrel, squirrelled
stanch (verb)
stationary (still)
stationery (paper)
staunch (adj)
storey (floor)
straitjacket and strait-laced,
    but straight-faced
stratagem
strategy
supersede
supervisor
Sunni, Sunnis
swap (not swop)
swathe (not swath)
synonym
Taliban (plural)
tariff
Tatar (not Tartar)
taoiseach (but prefer prime
    minister, or leader)
threshold
titbits
titillate
tonton-macoutes

tormentor
tortuous
trade union, trade unions
    (but Trades Union
    Congress)
transatlantic
transferred, transferring
transpacific
travelled
tricolour
trouper (in old trouper)
tsar (not czar)
tyres
unnecessary
unparalleled
untrammelled
vaccinate
vacillate
vermilion
wacky
wagon (not waggon)
weasel, weaselly
whizz kid
wilful
wisteria
withhold
yarmulke (prefer to kippah)
yogurt
yoke (frame binding oxen)
yolk (yellow in egg)
zipcode

-able

debatable
dispensable
disputable
forgivable

imaginable
implacable
indescribable
indictable

indispensable
indistinguishable
lovable
missable
movable
ratable
salable (but prefer sellable)

tradable
unmissable
unmistakable
unshakable
unusable
usable

-eable

bridgeable
changeable
knowledgeable
likeable
manageable
noticeable

serviceable
sizeable
traceable
unenforceable
unpronounceable

-ible

accessible
convertible
digestible
dismissible
feasible
inadmissible

indestructible
investible
irresistible
permissible
submersible

If in doubt, consult Chambers or the OED. It is time well spent.

Glossary

adverb: a word that can modify a verb (*quickly*), an adjective (*extremely* tall) or another adverb (*extremely* quickly).

clause: a set of words containing a subject and a predicate. A basic clause consists of a noun and a verb: *Cats meow*. Adding various bits and pieces to the subject and predicate does not change the fact that with one subject and one predicate it is just one clause: *The numerous cats outside my window meow incessantly at night.*

conjunctions: the little words that link other pieces of a sentence together. The most common are *and*, *but* and *or*. *Subordinating conjunctions* such as *that* or *which* open a subordinate clause (see below).

direct object: typically, the recipient of the action of a verb (The family bought *the house*). It is usually a noun, but can be other things, including a clause (She learned *that she was pregnant*).

independent clause: a clause that can stand on its own grammatically, such as a simple sentence like *Cats meow*. A sentence can have more than one independent clause: *Cats meow and dogs bark.*

mood: a quality of a verb that indicates how it is to be understood. The most common mood is the indicative: Anna *is* a lawyer. Another mood is the subjunctive, which deals with suggestion, requirement, exhortation and the like: Anna's mother insisted that she *be* a lawyer.

noun: a word that can be the subject of a sentence (The *cat* jumped), the object (I saw the *cat*); can be made possessive (the *cat's* pyjamas); usually can be plural (two *cats*), etc. Nouns include "persons, places or things", but not all nouns are one of these. A noun can be abstract (*nothingness*), or an action in noun form (the *completion* of the project), for example.

noun phrase: a part of a sentence that can fulfil certain roles, like being the subject or direct object of a sentence. It includes at least one noun, as well as things that pertain to it like *the*, adjectives and prepositional phrases. *The black cat in the hat* is a noun phrase, which itself contains two other noun phrases: *the black cat* and *the hat*. But noun phrases can also be nothing more than a single noun (*cats*).

predicate: typically the part of a clause that offers some description of the subject, such as a quality, a description of an action performed by the subject, or some other situation involving it.

preposition: a word that describes relationships, often spatial ones (*on, near*). But some prepositional relationships are non-literal (He talked *about* the book) or simply fixed by custom (*different from* is more accepted than *different to*). Prepositions take a noun phrase to complete a *prepositional phrase* (*in the white room, with black curtains, at the station*).

relative clause: a kind of subordinate clause that modifies or singles out a noun: The cat *that he bought*, the house *that they lived in*, a date *which will live in infamy*, arrant nonsense *which I will not put up with*. A relative pronoun, such as *who, which* or *that*, often introduces these clauses. But it is frequently optional: *the house that Jack built* or just *the house Jack built*.

sentence: a grammatically complete string of words consisting of at least one independent clause, which in print begins with a capital letter and ends with a full stop, question mark or exclamation point.

subject: the part of nearly every English sentence that agrees with the verb, and is what the sentence is about. Usually, the subject is a noun and performs an action (*Steve* jumps). But the subject can be things besides nouns. It can even be a clause (*How you ever got to teach a course in anything* is totally amazing). And in passive sentences the subject is not the "do-er" but the "do-ee": *The ball* was kicked by the boy.

subordinate clause: a clause that does not stand alone but is part of a larger sentence, in a dependent role: He regretted *that they had bought a cat*; She said *that he maybe should have mentioned this earlier*.

tense: a quality of a verb having to do with when in time the action takes place, such as the present or past.

transitive, intransitive verbs: a transitive verb takes a direct object: *He bought the oboe*. A ditransitive verb also takes an indirect object, or recipient: *He gave his daughter the oboe*. An intransitive verb has no objects: *He smiled*. Some verbs can be both: *She practised* or *she practised the sonata*.

verb: a word that carries the core information of a clause or sentence. Prototypically, it is an action word (*kicks*) but it is not always (*is, seems*). Verbs change form depending on person (I *kick*, he *kicks*) and tense (*kick, kicked*).

voice: a quality of a verb that determines how the performer and recipient of action are arranged in a sentence. *The editor corrected the article's grammar* is in the usual, active voice, with the subject (the editor) also the agent of the verb *corrected*. But in the passive voice, these roles are swapped: *The article's grammar was corrected by the editor*. Note: passive and active are not tenses.

Acknowledgments

Applying the guidance in this book—that is, to write with short words that everyone uses—I really should avoid "acknowledgments". What these are are heartfelt "thanks".

The Economist has been a collective endeavour since 1843. Its lack of bylines is unusual in journalism, but we like to think it means that prima donnas are unwelcome (or unlikely to apply), while those willing to collaborate will thrive.

And so while no book is truly written alone, this one is less so than most. Though redrafted from beginning to end, it draws heavily, sometimes word-for-word, on the venerable first style guide, written primarily by John Grimond, who had a storied career at *The Economist* and was also the guardian of its style for many of those years. The late Steven Hugh-Jones, the original "Johnson" columnist in the 1990s, provided a great deal of input to Johnny's guide; he was exercised in particular by "may" and "might", and this book carries his fingerprints on that and many other entries. Ann Wroe expertly took over the leading role from Johnny, updating and adding to the guide over many years. She was an inexhaustible font of good sense as she combined this role with writing her magnificent obituaries, and her detailed comments on this version have been particularly helpful. To step into her shoes is not a task undertaken lightly.

Many other colleagues at *The Economist* have provided input into matters of style that have made their way into this book. Anton La Guardia, Patrick Lane, Ingrid Esling and Xan Smiley have been stalwart contributors. Others provided their expertise on specific questions. In business, finance, economics and science, contributors include Catherine Brahic, Geoff Carr, Tim Cross, Henry Curr, Patrick Foulis, Natasha Loder, Oliver Morton, Jason Palmer, Jan Piotrowski and Rachana Shanbhogue. Chapter 4 is particularly indebted to them. Helen Joyce and I developed an online writing course in which she provided, in particular, the guidance on editing that underpins Chapter 5.

All of the small but important complexities treated here—titles of nobility, renamed cities, foreign surname conventions, military ranks and such—are beyond the expertise of any one person. Gregg Carlstrom, Bruce Clark, John Hooper, Shashank Joshi, Christopher Lockwood, Roger McShane, James Miles, Leo Mirani, Nicolas Pelham, Michael Reid and others helped me make sense of them all. No guide can please everyone in these regards, but these colleagues have, I hope, helped forge a style that reconciles the (sometimes competing) goals of being respectful, accurate and readable.

Fiammetta Rocco championed the rebirth of the Johnson column, giving me time to think and write about nothing but language, a joy and a privilege. And Andy Miller provided wise and patient editing for many years, proving to me with every column that nobody is above editing. Tom Standage encouraged the creation of this new guide, and above all (not only in our organisational chart) Zanny Minton-Beddoes blessed the idea of refreshing and rephrasing our guidance. Ed Carr has repeatedly shared with me his wisdom on matters of style, and on other matters too.

Clare Grist Taylor of Profile has my gratitude for her patience improving this book, Paul Forty for his meticulous copy-edit and Andrew Franklin for championing the Economist Books series over the years.

Index